Hey You Don't Scare Me.... Anymore!

Lessons— Questions—Answers

By Dwight Thirkield

ISBN-13: 978-1721672219
ISBN-10: 1721672214

Design and Layout by Jim Hurley Graphics

Contents

Preface
My search for answers

This is my story of trying to figure out what I refer to as "this God business": what God is like if such a Being actually exists. It began as a series of short notes, which I scribbled down in a notebook over a period of fifteen years. These notes were written memories of events in my life that have formed my present beliefs. I took the notes and began writing this memoir, which assembles those notes into an account of how I have come to no longer fear God, a journey that began when I was four years old. It was then that I first heard the word God. When I blurted out "My God!" at lunch one day, I was admonished for doing so, though I never understood why. Then, in religious classes as an older child, I was taught about how this Being, whom I thought of as this "God guy," was jealous, vengeful and angry. I heard about Hell, where non-believers would go after death to spend an eternity being burned and suffering agonizing pain.

I always wondered if those teachings were true, and because I wondered, I felt like I was in big trouble with God and would be punished for not accepting what I had been told was true. Now, as I write this memoir, I am an old man. I have asked God to speak to me, and maybe we have communicated. I can't say so for sure. But I can say this: I'm not only not afraid, I'm not afraid to make that statement.

Some people may ridicule me for what I write because they, in their infinite and often arrogant wisdom, claim that there is no Creator or Supreme Being. To them I say, prove it! I don't care in the least if I am subjected to ridicule. If a Supreme Being created all that we humans are aware of, including ourselves, then that same God certainly could have arranged things so humans would not be able to find a conclusive answer to the question, "Does God exist?" It seems to me that if there is a Creator, Supreme Being or God then it must have existed for all time and so I have chosen to call this being Old One.

I'm sure there will also be people who say that I am possessed by the Devil because of what I have written. To them I would respond by asking, does any such Devil exist? In fact, there are religious groups that encourage and even urge their believers to threaten people who criticize, poke fun of, or decide to leave that system of belief. These groups would find people leaving by the millions if their leaders weren't threatening them or those they hold dear with torture, death, or harm. It would be very interesting to know how many people who claim to believe in a certain religion do so only because of threats of harm, expulsion, or banishment from a family or social group.

Considering the amount and intensity of religious persecution in the world, I suspect there are some people who will be so angered by what I have written that they might want to harm, torture, or even kill me and my family. Yet any set of beliefs is meaningless if it forces people to say that they believe in a certain religion and threatens them with unspeakable punishments or death if they dare to criticize or abandon those beliefs. Should any person or organized group threaten to harm me, those people whom I love, or anyone else unless I deny what I have written in these pages, I will agree to do so. Because I have stated this now denying it sometime in the future will be meaningless. Beliefs cannot be forced upon people by threats; pretending belief to escape punishment is much easier.

Writing this memoir occurred mostly bit by bit over a number of years. When I began writing it, I was seventy-nine years old, now I'm eighty-three, I have lived long enough to become what I am now, an old man. I have not written about this journey to tell readers that what they already believe is wrong, or that they should change their beliefs to resemble mine. I have written this because I have finally come to a concept of God that is satisfying and fulfilling to me: an omniscient Being and Creator who is eternal, infinite, genderless, and personal. If anyone should read this memoir and gain some benefit or comfort from what I have written herein, then I consider this writing to be of some value. Whatever anyone thinks of my beliefs does not matter to me. I will not be offended or upset by being told that I am wrong. I welcome discussion.

Part I
Becoming

Chapter 1
Who Am I?

Let me introduce myself. I don't consider myself to be sophisticated—far from it. I don't care about any sort of status symbol, whether it be rising to a higher position in the corporation where I was employed, or owning Rolex watches, fancy cars, and expensive clothing. The one suit that I own and the tie and shoes that go with it are the same ones I wore when I retired from a position in engineering sales at the end of 1994. I still have that suit but seldom wear it. It's still presentable but perhaps dated. I could care less. As the years have passed, those same old clothes are being brought out, brushed off, and worn to funerals more and more often. That's what happens as the years tick by: people with whom I interfaced during my life are cashing in their chips.

My wardrobe now consists mostly of shorts and T-shirts for summer, and jeans and sweatshirts for winter, which is just fine with me. I have a favorite, somewhat dressy, pullover sweatshirt, red with widely spaced, narrow black stripes. I have had that sweatshirt for close to twenty years. My wife, Vera, got it for me when I began building us a house. I needed some work clothes, so Vera shopped at a nearby Goodwill store and bought several sweatshirts that would serve the purpose. I liked that pullover so much it became my "dress-up" sweatshirt. I don't wear it very often, usually only if we go to lunch or dinner at a casual restaurant. It just won't wear out, much to my delight.

I chuckle about shopping at Goodwill because there are those in our family who won't go anywhere near a thrift store. I remember a friend who worked for the same large corporation I did, who always dressed very well and had many good-looking suits. Once, during a break from a training session, the two of us were making small talk. He was wearing a suit that I admired. I commented about his appearance—how he always was very well dressed—and asked if he had a favorite men's store. He let out a hearty laugh and said, "Absolutely! I buy all my clothes at Goodwill stores." He went on to say, "Many people give clothes away just because they want the 'latest style' or something new. You like this suit I'm wearing? It cost me twenty bucks plus another twenty to a lady who does tailoring to adjust the fit."

I have mixed feelings about buying from Goodwill stores. It's not that I am ashamed of patronizing them; I couldn't care less what other people will think of me if it becomes known that I shop there on occasion. I do wonder if it's fair to buy an item at a fraction of the original price when I could afford to buy the same item new. I worry that I might be depriving someone less fortunate than I of an item he or she couldn't afford to buy new; but then my patronage does benefit the Goodwill and its job-training programs just like anyone else's.

I'm neither rich nor poor compared to all people in the United States; I put myself somewhere around the middle. I can't afford to do or have anything I would like, and that's okay too. I consider myself to be very fortunate to be in my present situation. Compared to many others in this world, I am rich beyond their wildest dreams.

Now that I've described what I am like on the outside, I'll tell you a little about the inner me. I am easily stirred emotionally. I sometimes choke up and shed tears when witnessing, hearing of, or being involved in touching or tragic events. I don't understand why I react this way; it's just part of my psyche I suppose. My father was much the same way. He would sometimes quote from a moving poem or piece of literature, and his eyes would fill with tears. That's just the way I am. I'm not ashamed in the least of being that way. I feel things deeply. I'm not the only man who does this; I have seen big, tough soldiers, firemen and policemen shed tears. A photograph that I saw in Life Magazine when I was a small child is burned into my memory. In the photo was an elderly French gentleman, tears streaming down his cheeks as he watched German army formations march through the Arc de Triomphe.

I tend to form deep attachments, not only with family and friends but also with pets and with even wild creatures I meet in my yard. One of my favorite nonhuman friends was a small black and white dog that was a loyal and affectionate friend for the six or seven years he lived with us. My young boys and I fell in love with the puppy when we saw him at the pet store, and when the boys grew older and busier with school and all their other activities, the dog and I became close buddies. He would greet me each day when I came home and sit near me all evening. I called him Augie Doggie after a TV cartoon dog he resembled.

One day I came home to find that my pal had died that day. Blinded

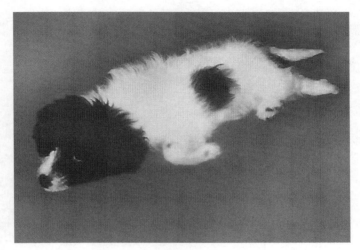

Augie Doggie

by tears, I stumbled out the back door and into the backyard. Lying there, covered by a towel, was my little buddy. I folded back the towel and touched him, and he was cold and stiff. I knelt there stroking his soft, curly fur sobbing as if I would never stop. Finally, I got up and went into the house, changed into yardwork clothes and went out into the backyard and got a shovel. I looked around the backyard to decide on a spot for my little buddy's grave, found a spot in a flower bed near some shrubs, and began digging. As I dug my cheeks were wet with tears.

I dug slowly, delaying the burial. Finally, I knew I had to put my pal to rest. I couldn't bear to just drop him into the hole in the ground. I had to lay him down gently. The grave was so deep that I had to lie on my stomach so that I could carefully place his little body on the bottom of the grave. He was still wrapped in the towel that Vera had put over him. I laid him in the grave, pulled the towel back from his tiny body, and stroked his fur. Finally, I covered him again with the towel, took a handful of earth and gently sprinkled it on the little towel-covered form. I took another handful of earth and did the same. I cried as I put another handful of earth over him. I filled his grave like that: a handful at a time

Front

Back

House on the hill in the woods which I built

until there was no more earth or tears left.

And then there was the hummingbird. We were living in the country about thirty miles southeast of Seattle, Washington. Our house was on five acres. Four acres were steeply sloped down behind the backyard and wooded, with large Douglas firs, hemlocks, cedars, vine and big leaf maples and alders. Black-tailed deer often wandered through our yard and dined on many of the flowers and vegetables that Vera enjoyed planting and nurturing through the summer months. When she would see the deer happily munching on some flowers that had just begun to bloom, she would pound on a window or stamp her feet on the deck to

14

scare them away; but it was a losing battle, so she tried to plant species the deer didn't care for. It was a love/hate relationship with the deer, though not really hate so much as good-sized irritation. But when a momma deer would appear with two spotted fawns following her, momma deer and her twins were allowed to eat whatever they wanted.

We loved the variety of birds that visited. There were loud-mouthed Steller's jays, flickers, towhees, juncos, sparrows, black-headed grosbeaks, evening grosbeaks, red-headed woodpeckers, and once in a great while a pileated woodpecker. We took a particular liking to the goldfinches and the hummingbirds, which we called "hummers." For several years we hung out two finch feeders, with six feeding positions on each one, and filled them with thistle seed. Sometimes we were fascinated to see both finch feeders with all feeding positions occupied and maybe two or three goldfinches waiting for a vacancy.

The goldfinches were social birds; not so the hummingbirds. The hummers were very territorial. We hung hummingbird feeders in several locations. If a hummer staked a claim to a feeder and another hummer approached it, a hummingbird aerial battle immediately followed—a battle so fast and furious that it started and ended in one or two seconds. The hummers became so accustomed to the location of the feeder that when one was taken in to be cleaned and refilled, they would hover and wait for it to be put back, sometimes starting to feed even before it had been settled onto the hook. Those tiny hummingbirds weren't the slightest bit afraid of me.

One evening in early summer I arrived at about 9:30. The outside lights hadn't come on; twilight still lingered. Sensing that Vera was feeling rather somber, I asked if something was wrong. She told me that one of our beloved hummingbirds had flown into a window and been killed. The hummers would sometimes fly into the window-pane near the feeder because they would see the reflection of the outdoors. Usually, they would recover in midair and dart away seemingly none the worse from the collision. Sometimes, they would fall to the deck, recover after a few minutes and fly away. But rarely, they wouldn't survive, as it had happened that evening. When a hummer died in that way, I could never just throw their tiny, beautiful bodies into the trash or toss them into the woods; I always felt I had to give them a burial. I wanted, maybe needed, to grieve and mourn the demise of these amazing creatures.

So, I changed into yard-work clothes, found my battery-powered lantern, went out on the deck and picked up Vera's garden trowel from the place where she kept it. I went to the deck railing where Vera had put the body and covered it with a paper towel. After uncovering the wee form, I shined my light on it and saw that it was a female Rufous hummingbird. Her back was green with a pattern on each feather of black and gray that resembled an eye; her feathers were iridescent in the lamplight. I marveled at how this tiny creature, with her brain the size of a pea, could perform the aerial feats of hovering, flying forward, backward, left, right, upside down, engaging in aerial combat and remembering the feeder location, just to mention a few of her capabilities.

I found a spot for her grave between two gorgeous sword ferns near a small goldfish pond. In the dusky twilight I carried her wrapped in the paper towel to the grave site and gently laid her down. Using the garden trowel, I dug her tiny grave, it didn't take but a few scoops with the hand trowel, she was so tiny. Lifting the lantern high to light the area, I spotted a bracken fern nearby and picked some of the small fronds to line the grave. Then, I laid her on the fronds lining her grave. Tears were streaming down my cheeks as I covered her with fronds. When her tiny form was covered with fronds, I picked up handfuls of soil and let it sift slowly through my fingers, handful after handful until I had no more soil. I gently patted the soil and placed a small, somewhat square-shaped stone on top as a marker for her grave. I rose from my kneeling position and walked back into the house. The hummingbird's funeral was over.

I haven't told you everything about my inner life. Often when I'm alone, often in nature or flying above the clouds, I ask Old One questions, even though I'm not absolutely certain that a Supreme Being actually exists. I am uncomfortable with the word God, maybe because of the admonishment I received at age four when I blurted out to my parents and sisters, "My God, look!" when I wanted their attention. In the many different religions of the world, the Creator or Supreme Being has been called by many different names: God, Yahweh, Allah, Jesus Christ, Baal, Ahura Mazda, the Great Spirit, and El-Shaddai, to name a few. I call the Creator Old One or It.

The famous scientist, Albert Einstein, who was Jewish by birth but did not practice the faith, referred to the Creator as the "Old One." I choose to use Einstein's name for God because the Creator must have existed for all eternity and is therefore infinitely old. (Many religions believe in a Creator that has existed throughout time and who knows everything: past, present, and future.) For Old One there is no time because, with the knowledge of all events throughout eternity, infinite time, everything is happening at once. It's different for us mortals, who are bound by time. As John Archibald Wheeler, an American Physicist, put it, "Time is what keeps everything from happening at once."

And so, Old One has knowledge of all events, including those of which humans are aware, all of what is past and future for humans, and an infinity of other happenings humans neither know of nor can even imagine. Old One possesses an intelligence far beyond that which the human mind can comprehend. No wonder it is difficult to believe in such a Being. One must choose to believe in a Supreme Being because Its existence can't be proven. Perhaps that was deliberate on Old One's part. If Old One created the universe and all living things, then Old One has the ability to mystify humanity.

During my life, I have discussed religion with many people that I have met. There have been those of many different beliefs: Catholics, Episcopalians, Seventh Day Adventists, Mormons, Baptists, Buddhists, Methodists, Baha'i, Zoroastrians, Hindus, Jews, Muslims, and probably others who have slipped my aged memory. I always enjoyed these discussions, often they were fascinating to me. Usually it was I who started them. The discussions never became hostile or angry; it takes two to start a fight. Although some people were quite vehement in insisting that their belief was the only one that was true and correct; I never argued with those with whom I conversed—not even if, in my private thoughts, I disagreed with some or all of their stated beliefs. I simply listened and sometimes asked questions. Some people were only interested in telling me what they believed: why theirs was the only true religion, and that if I didn't follow their religion, I was going to Hell for all eternity. Some people would ask what I believed and why. Although some of them would tell me how wrong I was, with others there would be a wonderful exchange of thoughts. I always took something away from these conversations that made me ponder the concept of religion and a Creator. Occasionally, the person who had listened to my beliefs would say that he or she had gained something from the discussion. I know I always did.

Often, I have wondered what Old One, God the Creator must be like—that is, if God exists—and I have come to believe that such a Being must be far beyond our capability to fully understand or accurately imagine. Imagine having the intelligence and ability to create the universe which we humans perceive! This Creator must have complete self-control. Does the Creator become angry? Anger is an emotion that humans experience when something happens that displeases them. Old One must be far beyond the human failing of becoming angry. I have come to believe that Old One never takes offense by what we humans do, but rather is like a loving and patient parent. A child often may sometimes say or do things that offend, disappoint, shock, or embarrass a parent, but a wise and compassionate parent realizes that the child is young, still learning and has not yet acquired enough knowledge to understand and cope with various situations.

And so, I believe that Old One views human behavior with total understanding, tolerance and probably sadness when seeing people harm themselves or others. Old One, I believe, is not in any way offended

Me, Mother, sisters MaryBelle and Lueza Denise

With trophy brown trout 1945 or 46

Age 13

My Life- Toddler to Old Man

Age 19

Age 34

Age 56

Age 83 Old man

by humans thinking or saying that they are unsure of Its existence. If anything, Old One appreciates their honesty and prefers that they not be fearful that Old One will be angry with them for being uncertain.

Chapter 2

Flashback! God: Something to Fear?

He had done something terrible, but he didn't know what it was. His mother, father and older sisters stared at him. They had gasped, open mouthed. He just wanted to disappear. That was the first time in his life that he had "bumped into God," so to speak. It was the summer of 1939. He was four years old.

Someone had gotten him a gift, a very simple kite consisting of two crossed sticks and a paper part with strings around the edges that snapped into slots in the ends of the sticks. One of his older sisters had put it together for him. Then it was time to fly the kite, but where was the string? There was no kite string. His sisters had found some short pieces of string and tied them together, but still there wasn't nearly enough string to get the kite very high into the air. When he was called to lunch, he went feeling disappointed yet determined. He sat at the table bursting with excitement at the thought of the kite soaring high into the cloudless blue sky of that gorgeous summer day. He gobbled down his lunch, so he could dig through drawers and other nooks and crannies where he might find string.

He was so excited when he found a ball of string! To his four-year-old mind, it was just what was needed to fly the kite. Gleefully, he ran back into the dining room where his parents and sisters were still seated at the table, held up the ball of string and shouted, "My God, look!" When he said that, they gasped and stared at him in a way that made him want to hide. One of his parents said in a very harsh tone that what he said was not nice, but he didn't understand what was wrong with saying "God." He crawled under the chair where he had eaten his lunch and curled into a fetal ball. That little boy was me, so many years ago. Yet the memory remains so clear in my mind; huddling under the chair seat, I felt terribly afraid and puzzled. I didn't know what I had done wrong. I only knew that my parents were angry with me and I didn't know why.

After all these many years that have passed, I still can't understand why I blurted out, "My God, look!" I don't remember ever hearing the word God before I blurted it out. That shocked and disapproving response to "my God" was the beginning of my uneasiness with God.

*****

I had a Christian religious upbringing of sorts. I was read to from the King James Version of the Bible, but I always had doubts about God's existence, even as a small child. Once, when I was about eight or nine years old, I asked my mother if it was really true what I'd been told about God. Her response was to appear a little angry, but mostly shocked, and gasp, "Why, don't you believe?" Although my response was "Oh yes! I believe, I believe," I really didn't. I only knew that if I didn't say that, I would be in trouble. At that age I had no idea of what to believe. After that, I never let on again to either parent that I doubted the Bible stories, but I had a nagging, guilty feeling that the biblical God would be angry with me and would punish me if He knew that I doubted His existence. Why wouldn't anyone have this feeling of guilt, particularly a child? I remember being taught that God becomes angry and is jealous; why wouldn't a child feel guilt and fear?

My mother, sisters and I attended the Episcopal Church in the small town in upstate New York where we lived. Our father would sometimes drive us to church but not attend with us. I had forgotten that until many years later during a conversation with my sister Lueza, discussing our childhood. She was then writing her own memoir. She said that when she had asked our father why he didn't go to church with the rest of the family, his answer was: "I pray in the woods."

When I reached the age of twelve or thirteen my mother told me that I was to be "confirmed." I had to learn and recite to the priest statements about what I believed so that I could be confirmed. I didn't know what those statements meant; I just knew I had to memorize them to avoid a huge argument with my mother. After I was confirmed, I participated in the rituals and recited the passages I had been required to memorize, but I still didn't understand the meaning of the words I recited. Compliance was much easier than refusing to participate at that time of my life, my early teenage years. Participation was forced upon me to by my parents, mostly by my mother, but to some degree because of our social circle.

I remember a sermon I listened to one Sunday when I was twelve or thirteen years old. The priest, Father Truesdale, was talking about the evils of fornication. I didn't know what the word meant. Sex was not mentioned in my home; most of my sex education came from the other kids in school. I think the priest thought he should say that fornication was evil because another boy and I were about the age when thoughts of sex were entering our heads. I laugh now when I realize that it was years before I ever figured out what the word fornication meant. I had learned only the four-letter words, and I didn't know for certain that what the kids in school told me those words meant was actually true. Only a few years earlier my family had told me that "the Stork" brought babies. My father never gave me "the talk" about the birds and the bees. I remember my father feeling my hands, checking to see if they were sweaty, and telling me, "Don't abuse yourself." Again, I didn't know what he meant by that. So much for sex education.

Back in the late 1940s and early 1950s when I was still a child and teenager, religious education was loosely affiliated with the public school. Once each week children would be ushered from the public school to one of the two churches, Protestant or Catholic, for religious instruction. We hardly knew any other religions existed. Volunteer ladies from each church were the teachers. We were graded on how well we memorized and recited various Christian religious teachings, including the Lord's Prayer and the Ten Commandments. The volunteer lady teachers would meet with parents and discuss a child's performance. I tried to do well, so that I didn't get into trouble with either the teachers or my parents. I remember being taught that God is jealous, angry, and vengeful and that after a person dies, anyone who hasn't believed what the Christian Bible teaches will spend eternity in a terrible place called Hell, where everyone suffers by being burned!

Other religions, including Judaism, Islam, Buddhism, Hinduism, were briefly mentioned in one of the public-school classes, but we were taught hardly anything of what these other religions believed.

For most of my life I had a nagging uneasiness that God would punish me for doubting what I had been taught about Christianity, the only "true" religion. Now, at this "downstream" point in my life, I no longer fear God. What I write herein is how I have come to shed this cloud of fear that hung over me for most of my life. Now, I am no longer afraid to think or say that I am not certain. I have, in my innermost thoughts, asked God, Old One, to talk with me, and I think that maybe God has, but I can't say without any doubt that God and I have conversed.

Chapter 3
The Beating

My parents, Eden Buckley Thirkield and Constance Ingham Harris Thirkield, were honest, decent people, who tried to keep me on what they deemed to be the right path during my growing-up years. My mother was born on the first of July, 1897, in the borough of Staten Island, New York City. Her father and grandfather had been successful in banking, and she had grown up in a household with servants. She had been sent to a private prep school and went on to Oberlin College in Ohio, where she and my father met. My father, who was born on 19 April, 1892, in Delaware, Ohio, was nearly five years older than my mother.

It's interesting how their paths crossed in Oberlin, Ohio. The youngest of my father's three much older sisters, Amanda Pearl, always called Pearlie, married Phillip Sherman, who was a professor of English literature at Oberlin College, from which my mother graduated, and my parents happened to meet when my father came to visit his sister.

My parents were married in 1920. The ceremony was performed by my father's uncle, Wilbur Patterson Thirkield, a bishop in the Methodist Episcopal Church. In 1925 my mother had received an inheritance and allowed my father to manage it. He dabbled in the stock market using my mother's money. He only had two jobs during my childhood and teen years until I enlisted in the Air Force at seventeen. During 1943 he was Assistant to the Comptroller of New York City, but that position ended when the Comptroller was defeated in the next election. In the late 1940s, he worked with a municipal consulting firm. I don't know why he lost that position. The reason my father gave was that one of the partners who disliked him, convinced the others that he was not doing the job effectively, and made it so unpleasant for him that he finally resigned. My father sued the firm for money he felt the firm owed to him. The lawsuit dragged on for years until it was ultimately settled for a small fraction of what he claimed he was owed. I describe my father as a wannabe who didn't know how-to be. I think he had a brilliant mind but, like many people of high intelligence, had great difficulty accepting an opinion differing from his own.

My father came from a family of pioneers who moved from Brownsville, Pennsylvania, to Franklin, Ohio, in 1815. At that time Franklin was a frontier community on the Great Miami River north of Cincinnati and about twenty-five miles south of Dayton. My father's great-uncle opened a dry goods store in 1825. My great-grandfather began working in the store in 1840 and eventually became the sole owner. My grandfather, George Thirkield, was the firstborn son, the crown prince, so to speak, for the eldest son was usually destined to take over the business. He did work in the store, but something happened that put an end to it. Whatever it was is a deep, dark, family secret. Grandpa George and his family left or were banished from Franklin and moved to Delaware, Ohio, in the early 1880s. Delaware and Franklin are separated

My parents 1939

by about 150 miles, a considerable distance at that time.

I have delved into my genealogy because I wondered why my grandfather and family were exiled to Delaware, Ohio. Besides Amanda Pearl, born in 1878, my father had two other much older sisters: Charlotte Balentine, born in 1874 and Henrietta Boise (always known as Jeanette), born in 1876. Jeanette never married and lived with us. In exploring my genealogy, I found the 1940 census—and may have dug up an unbelievable skeleton! The census page lists my father, my mother, my sisters, and—this is what is extremely interesting—Jeanette, was listed under relationship to the head-of-household as daughter, which was crossed out and mother written in, her age entered correctly. Was "Aunt" Jeanette actually "Grandma" Jeanette? If so, how so? A teenage affair? Rape? Incest? I have found only dead ends in my efforts to learn the answer. Was this woman, sixteen years older than my father, actually his mother, a grandmother to my sisters and me? In addition to the potential skeletons in the ancestral closet are the unanswered questions about my father and the shaping influences on his personality.

My parents may have come from similar backgrounds, but in temperament they were quite different. My mother was quite soft-spoken and rather easygoing. My father, however, was quite the opposite: he had a hair-trigger temper, and a thunder-loud voice with which he bellowed about whatever displeased him. If he wasn't angry about something, he often seemed to be in a sour mood. He often wasn't pleasant or fun to be around. I was afraid of him much of the time, and I learned once how violent he could be.

It was the first day of the school year September 1945. I was ten years old. The first day of school in the fall was always a half day. I asked my mother if I could ride my bike to school and then stay in town and play with friends in the afternoon. Mom gave permission and told me to have fun and to be home by five-thirty to be ready for dinner at six. Too busy having fun with my friends, I lost track of time, so I didn't get home on time. When I noticed that daylight was turning into dusk and looked for my bike to ride home, some older kids had hidden it. I spoke to the kids who had hidden my bike, telling them that I had to get home, but they jeered, laughed and taunted me, asking what I was going do about it?'

Then, my father drove up and growled at me to get home. I tried to tell him that the bigger kids had hidden my bike, but he wouldn't listen and started to yell at me. When the bigger kids saw that my father was there, they brought my bike to me. I opened the car door to put my bike in the back seat, but my father snarled at me to ride my bike home. Then, much to my embarrassment, he followed close behind me the entire mile and a half to our home. We had to go right down the main street of the town. People stared. I was mortified, but the worst was yet to come. When I was almost home, my father sped up and pulled alongside me, rolled down the window on the passenger side and ordered me to go to the barn; then, he sped up and turned into the driveway to the barn. By then daylight was almost gone. A dusky, eerie twilight was all that remained.

As I approached the open barn door, I could dimly see him, waiting for me. "Get in here," he growled. Trembling with fear, I shuffled over to him. He roughly grabbed my right shoulder with his left hand and squeezed hard enough that it hurt badly. He held a stick in his right hand. I recognized the stick because I had cut it from a longer stick of pine, one-by-two, while building a mockup airplane cockpit in which to pretend-fly airplanes. I had cut it to eighteen and a half inches long to use as the control stick in my make-believe airplane cockpit. He banged the stick back and forth against a wooden box, and the sharp sounds of it hitting the box made me jump. "This should do it!" he snarled.

I have never forgotten the brutal beating he inflicted upon me, his son, a ten-year-old boy, that dusky evening in the barn. He squeezed my shoulder harder and hit me with that stick, between my belt and knees, both sides, forehand and backhand, while all the time roaring in his loud voice telling me what a rotten child I was. Frozen in terror, I neither cried nor screamed.

Finally, he must have decided he had beaten me enough and roared for me to go to the house.

As I walked, half-stumbling because of the pain, back toward the house, I recalled the Bible story of how Abraham was commanded by God to kill his son Isaac, but God had stayed his hand at the last moment. Was my father told by God to beat me to death but then God stopped him?

Mother saw me when I came through the door and told me to go take a bath. She must have been upset that I had not come home on time. I had stripped, run bath water, and was about to get into the bathtub when Mother knocked. I mumbled, something. She came in and she saw the outside of my thighs, from my hips to my knees. They were ugly black and blue and in a few places the skin was nearly broken and bleeding. I still remember the expression on my mother's face—a look of shock and disbelief.

"Did he do this to you?" she asked.

I nodded yes. My voice wouldn't work, I couldn't speak.

I must have been in a state of shock. I suppose I couldn't speak because of the trauma, both physical and mental.

The ugly black and blue marks on my thighs from my waist down to my knees made me somewhat of a "macho" kid at school. I remember getting into gym clothes when another boy saw the bruises. His eyes almost bugged out and he seemed to gasp as he asked, "What happened to you?" I recall acting sort of nonchalant and saying, "My old man beat the shit out of me."

I wonder still, these many years later, what that beating incident did to my psyche. Why do I still choke up, recalling it, as I write about it so many years later? I must have buried it in the furthest depths of my mind because I don't remember thinking of it for forty years.

My wife, Vera, was gone to an evening class. The youngest kids were in bed and the oldest away living on his own. I was watching some TV show in which there were adults discussing abuse that they had suffered as children. Their stories—tales of pure horror! Their abuse continued for years and was much worse than that one time my father beat me. Yet the memory of my father beating me suddenly burst out of the depths of my memory. I find myself sobbing uncontrollably as I write about it now.

I wonder about my father's upbringing. What had shaped his personality in such a way that he would do that to his son? Why did he beat me so brutally? I now wish I had asked him that question after I had become an adult and was responsibly caring for a family. I suspect that if I had brought up the subject, he would have burst into tears and blubbered over and over that he was sorry. I think he wanted to be a good father but didn't know how. I'm certain that he had some serious mental hang-ups. Numerous times during my childhood and early teenage years my father would suddenly leave for an unspecified period of time "on business," but the rest of the family never knew what was meant by "business."

Many years later after my father had died, my mother told me that she suspected that he was a homosexual. Were his "business trips" excuses to meet with another man? If this were true it might explain his hang-ups; homosexuality was totally unacceptable at that time. If he was a homosexual, he was probably beset with feelings of guilt and self-hatred, which possibly accounted for his moodiness and explosive temper.

Chapter 4
The Dream of Flying

As I grew into my teenage years, I had difficult times. My parents had dreams for me that were not the same as those I had for myself. Their plans were that I graduate from a good prep school, get into an Ivy League university, and become a doctor, lawyer, banker, or—what I think was my father's dream—work for Merrill Lynch, make tons of money and give him bragging rights about his fantastic son. Those occupations were not my dream. I had fallen in love with airplanes and the dream of flying when I was four years old. Eventually, much later in life, I did fly airplanes as a paid (not much) job, and that was the only time in my life that I couldn't wait to go to my job. In fact, I didn't consider it work.

My parents did not want me to pursue a career flying airplanes. I think there were two reasons why they objected so strongly. They were both born in the 1890s—my father in 1892 and my mother in 1897—before there was such a thing as an airplane. They thought flying an airplane was certain to result in a crash and my being killed; yet, as my father would say (quite correctly), flying was the safest means of travel. Of course, that adage applied to airline flying, not to the "little" airplanes in which a beginning pilot first takes lessons.

The other reason they objected to my dream of flying was that if their son became an airline pilot, they wouldn't have the bragging rights that mattered to them. They were snobs and dreamed of telling people of their son, the doctor, the lawyer, or the vice-president of a large, well-known bank. My mother used to say to me: "Be somebody, be a vice president!" Until I was ten or eleven years old, if some adult, other than my parents, asked me what I wanted to be when I grew up, and I would reply that I wanted to fly airplanes, my mother would sort of snicker and say, "He'll get over that silly idea." After that happened just a few times, I didn't want to be laughed at anymore. From then on, if I were asked the same question, I would lie and name some occupation that pleased my mother, so she wouldn't tee-he about me and say that what I wanted to do was silly. If I said it while at the dinner table at home, both my aunts, my father's elder sisters who lived with us, would giggle and say, "That's so silly! Your father said he wanted to be a railroad engineer, but he got over that crazy notion. Besides if God had meant for man to fly, He would have put wings on him."

Many years later I worked with a gentleman who had been a naval fighter pilot during World War II. I told him what my aunt said about God and flying. He laughed and said, "Well, if that's true, God didn't mean for people to ride in cars or even wagons or he would have put wheels on them." If I had said that in response to my aunt's comments, it would have been considered "disrespectful," and I would have gotten into trouble. In the home where I grew up, pointing out that a grownup was wrong about something wasn't a smart thing to do—even if they were wrong. I do wonder what their response would have been!

My eldest sister, Mary Belle, eight years older than I, decided that she wanted to become a nurse. Oh, the discussions around the dinner table during which our parents did all they could to discourage her from pursuing that goal! Their plan for Mary Belle was that she would attend an Ivy League college, Smith or maybe Vassar. (My Aunt Rae, our mother's eldest sister, had graduated from Vassar.) After graduation Mary Belle was to marry a nice young man from the right social class, give them grandchildren, and live happily ever after.

Our parents had firm plans for Mary Belle and me to land the right job or spouse and impress their friends and family. To varying degrees, we both rebelled against those plans, but I never gave up half-heartedly trying to please our parents. Mary Belle had more backbone than I did and accomplished what she had chosen to do. She followed and achieved her dream of becoming a nurse.

My next elder sister, Lueza, seemed to toe the line and want the same goals that our parents had for each of the three of us. Much later in life she told me that she just figured out how to play the game.

It seems that my parents did everything they could to discourage me from my pursuing my dream, even long after I had grown up and left my childhood home. Still halfway trying to please them, I did realize that I had made some stupid mistakes as a teenager. For whatever reason, I gave up pursuing my dream of becoming an airline pilot and somewhat caved in to their effort to run my life even into adulthood. Now, at my advanced age, I resent my parents not only for discouraging me but also for putting obstacles in my way of achieving my dream of becoming an airline pilot. Were they concerned that they would be considered failures by their respected friends and family members if their son became an airline pilot instead of a banker, lawyer, or doctor? Well, I did okay as far as earning a living went but never came near what they dreamed of my becoming.

I was deeply touched when I met a gentleman who encouraged his son to pursue a dream that many parents would consider to be a childish fantasy. I was driving on a weekday during business hours in a business sector of a Seattle suburb, not far from my home. I reached up to reposition my eyeglasses and a lens fell out. As luck would have it, I recalled that just a few blocks ahead there was an optical shop I had driven past many times but had never patronized before. How convenient, I thought. I pulled into a parking place in front of the shop, got out of my car and entered. No other customers were there. An older gentleman approached the front counter from a room behind. I explained the situation, and he offered to do the repair immediately. Being the social creature that I am, I asked if he would mind if I watched while he completed the repair.

"Sure," he said, "Come on back."

I followed him to the small shop room in back. I enjoy very much hearing accounts of people's lives, especially of their families. He was not a young man, being perhaps in his late fifties or early sixties. I asked if he had children, and he replied that he had one child, a son. When I asked what his son did and where he lived, a faint smile crossed his face.

"He lives in Wyoming and he's a cowboy."

I was intrigued by his answer because his response was so unexpected. How, I wondered, could a child who was raised in a suburban setting so close to a large urban area ended up being a cowboy. Eager to hear this story, I asked the man putting my glasses back together how his son had become a cowboy.

He seemed only too pleased to tell me. He said that from the time his son was little more than a toddler, he had always said he wanted to be a cowboy. I thought his next words were a wonderful revelation of the love this man had for his child.

"I always encouraged him to be a cowboy if that was what he really wanted. After he finished high school he headed for cattle ranch country: Montana, Wyoming, and Colorado. He went to one ranch after another until he found a rancher willing to give this eager young kid a chance. That was twenty-five years ago, and now he's the ranch manager. He found a good woman who loved that life, and together they share the life that my son said he always wanted."

What a beautiful story! How many parents would not laugh at the boy who said he wanted to be a cowboy, tell him it was silly and that he would get over that childish notion? It particularly resonates with me because of how my parents not only snickered about my wanting to become an airline pilot but actually put obstacles in the way of my pursuing that career.

Chapter 5
School Years

Fortunately, my parents didn't try to squelch my interest in music. For my twelfth birthday I asked for and was given a guitar, a much used (and abused) guitar. It was good enough for a starter, and in a short time I had learned a few chords, enough to accompany myself when singing simple folk songs, like "Red River Valley," "Darling Nellie Gray," and "You Are My Sunshine," that needed maybe three chords to sound passable. I had the inborn gift to hear which chords fit these simple melodies without anyone having to teach me. Mother bought me a book of chords, and I worked at learning more chords and how to fit them into the popular songs of the late 1940s. My mother had graduated from Oberlin College where she studied piano. She would help me work out the chords for pop songs of that time, which were more complicated.

Only two other boys in the school played guitar, and they were pretty much stuck on songs with three or four chords. My musical ability helped me become a star in that little school. I had never been very good at basketball or baseball, the only two sports that were offered. I had no brothers from which to learn, and in all my childhood and teenage years, my father, who was always "too busy" or away from home for an unspecified length of time "on business," played catch with me once for maybe ten minutes. Playing guitar as well as I did tmade me into a "somebody." There were always other kids hanging around me when I played the guitar and sang.

The town where I lived from age three to seventeen was a very small rural community in upstate New York on the eastern edge of the Adirondack Mountains. The year-round population was maybe 1,000, but the number would swell to several thousand during mid-June through Labor Day while the "summer people" were there. The school was a two-story, brick building for grades kindergarten through twelve, with perhaps 250 kids in total. If I had been in my graduating class of

1952, there would have been eight graduating seniors.

The teachers were, for the most part, a revolving door, with

The home at Schroon Lake, New York where I lived from summer 1938 until March 1952

replacements arriving every year. A few—mostly teachers of the lower grades—were there for their entire teaching careers. There were two high school teachers that I still consider were very good: Harry Tucker, who taught Math, Physics and Chemistry, and Mildred (Millie) Bodin, who taught English, French and Latin. I got better than average grades without exerting much effort. I was able to coast along and, consequently, didn't develop good study habits, which caused me difficulties later when I realized I needed to further my education. I didn't enjoy high school classes very much other than science, which was to become a passionate interest later in my life.

My parents had always planned that I would go away to private school for some of my high school years. When I was fourteen and beginning my sophomore year of high school, I was sent to the Phillips Exeter Academy, in Exeter, New Hampshire. I didn't want to go; I didn't want to become a doctor, a lawyer or an investment banker. I wanted to become an airplane pilot, but I had learned not to tell my parents that. I have long wondered why I was admitted to Exeter, considering my grades weren't great. The fact that my Uncle Dwight went to Exeter may have carried some weight in my gaining admission. I now believe that I did have the intellectual capability to make it through Exeter, but I was very much unprepared to go there, both academically and socially. While I was there, I didn't try my best; I saw some of the other boys hurriedly doing their homework at the last minute and followed those bad examples, instead of applying myself to do the best I could. I was very immature for my age.

After I had been at Exeter for about a month, another boy and I got into some mischief. The adult in charge asked who had done it. I confessed to being a part of it, but the other boy lied and didn't own up to his part. I was told that I would have to appear before a student disciplinary council. The punishment would have been something minor, perhaps not being allowed to go to the Saturday night movie for maybe a month. Since I didn't want to be there, I used the excuse that the other boy didn't share the blame, to run away and go back home. That's what I did: I ran away. I have often regretted that I didn't take advantage of that opportunity for a first-class education.

So, there I was, back at Schroon Lake Central School in my sophomore year, still playing the guitar and once again a star. My interest in schoolwork waned. I kind of slid through without much interest or effort.

The summer of 1950 an event occurred that lifted me to the peak of euphoria one day and then dropped me into the pits of bitter disappointment the next day. A young man named Lewis Fairfield, a World War II veteran who had grown up in Schroon Lake, had not been a pilot during World War II, but had used his GI Bill to learn to fly. Lewis was working at whatever flying job he could find to increase his logged flying hours. He was flying a two-place Taylorcraft seaplane for a resort owner, taking one person at a time for an airplane ride. This was 1950, so not that many people had ever been up in an airplane. He had taxied the Taylorcraft up to the public beach where I happened to be. I had known him for a few years, and he knew how crazy I was about airplanes and flying. He asked me if I wanted to ride with him between the resorts and beaches in search of passengers. His plan was to have me talk to people and try to sell others on going for a ride while he was taking a person for a ride. I thought I had died and gone to heaven! While the airplane was in transit between resorts, he would give me flight instruction. I faced only one hurdle, a big one: getting my parents' permission. He let me fly with him to the resort where the Taylorcraft was beached for the night. He told the owner of the resort (also the airplane owner) of his plan to take me along to sell rides. The resort owner agreed to this plan if I had my parents' permission. Lewis, whom everyone called Lew, dropped me off at my home and said that he would stop by the next morning at seven o'clock to pick me up if my parents approved the plan.

It was an hours-long battle with my parents to get them to allow me to do this, but finally they did. I was up with the birds the next morning, so eager to go that I could hardly contain my excitement. Lew stopped for me and drove us on to the resort. The plan for the day was to fly to Lake George—about a thirty-minute flight—to buy a very simple part that had to be replaced before he could fly paying passengers. I had read all that I could find about airplanes and flying and had sneaked in some other rides with pilots who let me handle the controls after I had showed them how much I knew.

Lew me fly the airplane except for the take-off and landing. He got the part and installed it. After that we flew to several, small lake resorts, where we landed and looked for paying passengers. About noon we went back to the base resort for lunch. My parents were there, pacing on the beach. When they asked if I was ready to go home with them, I replied, "Absolutely not!" They stayed on the beach nearby until we took off again to seek out paying passengers. We touched down at several parks and resorts. I sold a few people on going for a ride. As the daylight waned, we returned to the base resort. Then I learned that my parents had talked with the resort owner and that my flying was over. I was devastated. I don't remember what transpired after Lew dropped me off at home— probably a huge go-round with my parents. My disappointment likely has clouded my memory.

Chapter 6
Honkytonk Guitar Pickin'

I don't know if I wanted to "get even" with my parents for stopping me from flying, but during my junior year in high school I quit trying. I didn't do homework. I pretended to sleep in class, and wouldn't participate in class discussions. I don't recall consciously behaving that way to punish my parents. I did still play the guitar, and it likely was the cause of my going further astray.

There was another World War II vet in town by the name of Jim Winchell, a Mohawk Indian. He was twelve years older than me. A classmate of mine, Rita Nolette, quit school when she turned sixteen, and she and Jim Winchell got married. Jim was small, wiry, really good-looking, jet black hair and eyes, dazzling smile of white teeth which contrasted with his dark complexion. He was extremely gifted musically. He had begun playing fiddle for square dances when he was only seven years old. He also played the guitar, much better than I did, but we found we could make music together and we really clicked. He and some other local people had formed a band to play for square dances, and he asked me to join the band. Another battle with my parents ensued.

The band played in bars, grange halls, community centers, school dances—anywhere they could find a job (the word "gig" either hadn't been coined yet, or it wasn't used in that locale). I was only fifteen, but it was legal if I played without being paid. Finally, my parents gave in. When I first started with the band, it was on Friday and Saturday nights.

In February 1951 Jim was contacted by Leonard Monette. Monette didn't have much hair on his head, but what little he had was red, so he went by the nickname of Red. He lived in Mineville, a town about thirty miles away. At that time Red was working in the iron mines, but he didn't want to work there or at anything else, aside from playing music in honky-tonks. He had been in and out of the bottom of the music business for a few years and knew much more about the "tricks of the trade" than Jim or I did. He knew how to book jobs, how to promote a band, and how to get a radio slot on one of the two low-power stations in Plattsburgh, New York. Red formed a band with Jim and me, a trio actually. Red played stand-up bass, Jim the fiddle, which left me as guitar singer and square dance caller. It was called "Red Monette and his Barn Dance Gang." He booked jobs at honky-tonks for Friday and Saturday nights and Sunday afternoon and evening. He also got us a half-hour radio show on WEAV.

I thought I was on my way to the big time. We did the first radio show live. The second show and three or four after that were all taped, so I could hear myself—and when I did, I wanted to crawl into a hole and pull it in after me. I sounded absolutely awful. I sang on key quite well, but my enunciation was terrible! At least I was smart enough to realize that I had a long way to go. In subsequent taped shows I improved a lot, but never to my complete satisfaction. Then, I fell in love—at least as much in love as a fifteen-year-old can be. Red knew two sisters who sang together: a young married woman with a couple of kids and her younger sister who was my age. The younger sister and I thought we were in love. To top it off, now that I was sixteen, I could get my driver's license. Being in love and old enough to get my license were two epic events in my life.

I had to face another battle with my parents, but they caved in, and I got my driver's license. Now I could go see my new-found sweetheart and take her out. Sadly, the bandleader, Red, had no loyalty to anyone. He changed band members the way people change their underwear, but in his case, it was whenever the mood struck him. My friend Jim I were soon without a job in a band. During my short time with Red's band, I had met some of the other music makers in the area and sat in with their bands.

A friend and I were in Plattsburgh on a Sunday evening going to the honky-tonks. The drinking age in New York in 1951 was eighteen, and it was only sporadically enforced in those small towns. I also had acquired a phony driver's license that showed my age to be twenty. I had the family car, a new 1951 Dodge, four-door sedan. We were about to leave and head back home when the band took a break, and the bandleader called me over. He offered me a job playing in his band five nights a week plus Sunday afternoon. I don't know how I expected to take that job and still go to school, but I accepted and was to start in three days, a Wednesday.

We started the seventy-mile drive from Plattsburgh to Schroon Lake at about eleven o'clock in the evening. I quickly came up with a stupid plan: if I drove fast I could get to The Kitty Korner, a honky-tonk in Witherbee about fifty miles away, where my girlfriend would be with her sister and brother-in-law until it closed at midnight. I had about an hour to make it there, over two-lane country roads, of which fifteen miles was a very curvy, hilly, narrow road. My driving was crazy and way over the speed limit. I made it without crashing until the curvy, hilly, narrow road. When I came to a sharp corner, I ran the family car off the road into a swamp. It didn't damage the car much, but it would have to be pulled out by a tow truck. That road had hardly anyone living on it for several miles and no streetlights. It was so dark we could hardly see our feet.

Luck was with us. Two soldiers in a beater car came by and gave us a ride to the nearest town. I called home and told my father what had happened. He said to wait there and he would come. After another hour or so my father arrived and asked where the car was in the ditch. I told him, and he drove away to look over the situation, leaving my friend and I to wait for him to return. After the beating he had inflicted upon me six years before, I was terrified of what he might do to me. When he returned, he ordered my friend and me into the other family vehicle, a truck he used for hauling firewood. He drove back to Schroon Lake and let my friend out at his home and then drove on to ours. Not a word was spoken the entire trip. He never said he was glad that neither I nor my friend had been hurt or killed when I ran the car off the road. He parked in our driveway and ordered me to go into the house. Mother was waiting at the door. He stormed in and started roaring at me, saying how if I had only said I was sorry everything would have been okay. I tried to tell him that I was sorry, but he roared at me again and tried to grab me with one hand and hit me with the other.

Fearful of what he might do to me, I twisted away and ran out the front door and across the highway in front of our house. I was almost hit by a car. My father stopped to let it pass and then chased after me. I was no match for him in size. He was stocky, short, big-boned, very strong, and outweighed me by about seventy pounds, but I could outrun him. I didn't want to fight him anyway. I was sorry for what I had done and would have apologized if I had been given a chance. I hid where I could see if he came looking for me. I waited for a while, maybe half an hour, but he didn't try to look for me in the woods where I hid. I saw the truck leave and knew that my father had gone. The only thing I could think to do was to leave home.

I went back to the house and in through the front door. Mother was there, but before we could talk my father drove into the driveway, parked and stormed into the house. When he saw me, he started yelling again, but I interrupted him, screaming out that I would just leave home so he wouldn't have to put up with me. His response was to sneer at me and ask how I thought I could fend for myself. I responded by yelling that I had a job playing in a band and was quitting school and moving out. I don't understand to this day why my parents allowed me to do that.

I remember what was in my mind after that shouting match with my father. If he had taken me aside before the drive back to Schroon Lake and firmly but calmly said how disappointed he was that I had behaved so irresponsibly, and if he had told me that my driving privileges were taken away until I began working hard at my schoolwork, and that he would get me tutoring help if I needed it, I believe I would have gotten back on the right path. And looking back over an expanse of more than sixty years, I can't help adding another "if." If only my mother and father had held out the carrot of allowing me to take flying lessons in exchange for achieving lofty schoolwork goals, I would have busted my ass to accomplish whatever was asked of me. And if he had only told me that he was glad that neither me nor my buddy were hurt or killed. . . .

My Air Force buddy Bill Rose and me.
The only photo I have of my guitar pickin' career. On a TV show
while stationed in Alaska from November 1953 until November 1955.

Chapter 7
On My Own

My parents allowed me to quit school. I was just over sixteen years old. That same Monday morning I went to the school, told them I was quitting, and turned in my books. I hitch-hiked the seventy miles to Plattsburgh and checked in with the band leader, Russell LaTour. His brother Alden owned a large, old rundown house and he was fixing up the downstairs into an apartment. There was a tiny room up an outside staircase that he rented to me for three dollars a week.

The room was about ten by ten, large enough for a double bed and not much else. The walls were covered with flattened cardboard boxes. The light fixture was a one-foot-long piece of one-half-inch pipe with a lightbulb on one end, a wire hanging out with a plug-in, and no light switch; just plug it into the one wall plug when light was wanted and stick the pipe into a hole in the cardboard. The "closet" was a few nails on the walls for hangers. The LaTour brothers' mother lived in a small house between Alden's house and Lake Champlain. I remember the address: 26 Scomotion Avenue. Directly across from Alden's "apartment house" was the city dump. I didn't have a bathroom with my room, so I had to use the one in the mother's house.

At the end of Scomotion Avenue, where it ended at the main road north out of Plattsburgh, was one of the two honky-tonks where we played music. It had previously been named "The Sit and Spit" and then "The Bucket of Blood." We played there Friday, Saturday, Sunday nights from eight to twelve and Sunday afternoons from two to six. Wednesday and Thursday nights, we played at a nightclub in a residential neighborhood called "The Lido Club." If the band played one minute after midnight, the neighbors would call the police to complain; the police would enter the place and everyone would be chased out. The Lido had a bar just inside the front entrance with a few tables. Through a wide door going on back were the dance floor, tables and a small stage. A rather bizarre incident happened one night at The Lido Club. When the band took a break, we headed for the men's room and then to the bar to grab a beer. When I went to the bar all the stools were taken, so I leaned in between two guys to order a beer. One of them turned to face me and I almost passed out. The guy facing me was the state trooper from my hometown, wearing civilian clothes. I thought I was in big trouble, but he greeted me with a big smile—and paid for my beer!

The band, if you could call it that, was only three pieces most of the time. Russell, who went by the name Rusty, played the accordion and sang. I played rhythm guitar and sang, and Ken Bouvier played rhythm guitar. Other local musicians would sometimes either drop by or sit in. I had learned many more chords than most of the other guitar players in the area. I could play some of the popular songs of that time, whereas the other guitar players were lost after a few major chords. I kind of stood out for that reason. There was one guitar player who was way beyond me: Curly Plummer. I couldn't begin to keep up with him. His problem was that he wasn't dependable. Sometimes he just wouldn't show up.

I had fun. I loved performing and I still do. I show up at open mikes occasionally. And I had my own car. I wish I had taken good care of it and still had it today. It was a 1939, Cadillac, two-door convertible. It would be a very valuable classic if it were in pristine condition. I paid $175 for it.

I thought that I was quite the cool guy, driving around in my Caddy convertible with the top down. I would be in Plattsburgh from Wednesday afternoons through Monday morning. Then I would go back to my parents' house to do laundry. Monday and Tuesday evenings, I would go to Mineville where my girlfriend lived. I would take her to a movie in Ticonderoga. On the way back home, we would park and smooch. I was not a decent guy at that time in my life. I was stringing any girl along who would fall for my line of BS. I really did like the girl from Mineville, but it wasn't very long before my cheating ways got me caught.

Saturday nights the Mineville girl, her sister, sister's husband, and girlfriend would come to Plattsburgh to spend the evening in the honky-tonk where I was making music. They would usually get there after we started playing. So, I didn't expect them when they got there earlier one evening. I was sitting at a table with my back to the door, drinking beer and necking with a Plattsburgh girl. The Mineville girl came in with her girlfriend, saw me with the other girl, and walked out. That was the end of that romance.

Not long afterwards, I had finished the Sunday evening gig and hung out with the band mates at an all-night diner until about four in the morning. It was late June so daybreak was early. I decided to drive to my parents then instead of sleeping in my dump of a room. It was about a one-and-a-half- or two-hour drive at the speed limit. There was no freeway at that time, only a two-lane hilly, curvy road. So, I began the seventy-mile drive. The last one-half mile was up a gentle hill with a fairly sharp hilltop crest. Then it gently sloped downhill to my parents' house. It had been raining, but the rain had stopped, leaving the pavement wet. Darkness had morphed into early dusk. There were misty patches now and then. There were no streetlights. As I approached the crest of the hill I was not speeding. Out of a patch of mist a figure appeared in the middle of my lane; it was a Canadian guy on a very small motorcycle. The tail light was burned out. I locked up the brakes, and the Caddy slewed to the left. I knew that I should turn the wheel right to straighten out, but if I had I would have hit the ghostly figure; so, I turned the wheel to the left. The car did a half-rotation, skidded sideways across the on-coming lane, hit a power pole on the passenger side, sheared off the power pole, and came to rest over a low bank.

I had to report the accident. I figured that I was in a heap of trouble. My driver's license Junior Operator's License did not permit driving during the hours of darkness. I told the motorcycle guy that he had to go with me to report the accident. I got on the motorcycle behind him, and we rode back the mile or so into town to the State Police Station. I knew who would open the door when I rang the doorbell; the same state policeman that had bought me a beer in the Lido Club a few days before.

I had to appear before a Justice of the Peace for the offense of driving after dark. I was fined $5.00 and a report of my conviction for driving after dark was filed with the state. I knew what would happen; my license would be revoked. It took several months but in November I received the notice from the state to send in my license.

The Caddy convertible was history. My playing guitar in the honky-tonks was ended because the state cop put out the word to all law enforcement in the area to be on the lookout for me. He probably went somewhat easy on me because I told him that his buying me a beer was our secret.

I owed a small amount on the Caddy to the dealer where I had bought it. He took it back for what was owed and gave me a 1935, four-door Chevy that was a real junker; but at least I had wheels. During that time, I lived at home with my parents. I found a few gigs with my friend Jim Winchell in summer resorts where booze wasn't served so I was legal. I worked whatever odd job I could find. I dug foundation holes for seventy-five cents an hour for a business that was creating a theme park. I cut trees for pulp wood, which was trucked to the paper mill at Ticonderoga. The school year began. I went to the school and talked with the principal. I could go back to school, but I would have to repeat the entire junior year. I didn't want to do that, so I didn't go back to school. In retrospect, my thinking that I could go back to school as a senior was totally ridiculous; I had flunked all my courses because I didn't even try. More odd jobs. The months rolled by. By late fall I was back making music with my buddy Jim Winchell again. I think the state cop had forgotten about me. We were making music again in the honky-tonks in Mineville, thirty miles from Schroon Lake

Several of the guys a year or two older than me that I had been in school with had quit high school and enlisted in the Air Force. They came home on leave, and I asked them what jobs they were assigned.

Two of them had been sent to Basic Airplane Mechanics School. After finishing tech school, they were assigned to be flight engineers on small transport airplanes. That's what I wanted to do. As my seventeenth birthday neared, I told my parents that I wanted to join the Air Force. They agreed to sign the permission paper which was required when the person enlisting was seventeen; at eighteen no permission was required. So, on March 26th, 1952, I was sworn into the United States Air Force. I think my parents were relieved to see me gone; they probably thought the military would get me straightened out.

Chapter 8
Air Force Orders

Air Force basic training was at Sampson Air Force Base. It was a reactivated World War Two Naval training facility on Lake Seneca in western New York State, only about a three or four-hour drive from Schroon Lake. My next older sister, Lueza, was about to graduate from Wells College, a private, liberal-arts, women's college located in Aurora, New York on Lake Cayuga, the next finger lake to the east. Lueza had followed the path that our parents had hoped all their children would take. I was the "black sheep" of their three children. Even Mary Belle, my oldest sister by eight years who became a registered nurse, wasn't nearly the black sheep that I had become.

During all my drinking beer and carousing, I hadn't given much thought to what I now call "this God business," but I always felt a kind of nagging unease that God was angry with me because of my blurting out, "My God, look!" when the kite event happened. The Air Force, however, made some attempt to instill some religious interest, I suppose it could be called, in the basic recruits. One had to declare a religious preference and were given three choices at that time, Protestant, Catholic, or Jewish. Then, those of each group would be lectured to, or maybe it could be called "given a sermon," by a chaplain of their chosen denomination. At that time in my life, I didn't have any real concept of religion. Oh yes, I had been "confirmed." I had memorized and recited words that I didn't understand and participated in services and rites because I had been made to. Yet, after all that, I hadn't gotten over my unease that "God got really mad and would punish you."

I had a hard time during Basic Training. It began in late March, and the weather was cold with mixed rain and snow. Recruits were not coddled; physical training took place outdoors, which meant we all would become wet and cold. After a week of boot camp, I developed a severe ear infection which put me in the hospital for twenty-two days.

Out of the hospital, I was back to the start of basic training. By late June I had completed my training and was awaiting orders for my next assignment, which I hoped would be Airplane Mechanics School at Wichita Falls, Texas.

I wanted to be somehow associated with airplanes, preferably flying as a crew member; but it was not to be. One follows orders without question when in the military. The orders I received were a huge disappointment. I was ordered to Communications Center Specialist School at Francis E. Warren Air Force Base, Cheyenne, Wyoming, to be trained for a position that had nothing to do with airplanes.

One day I was on a truck with a group of other guys. We had been on some clean-up job, what was called "shit detail," probably picking up trash, sweeping sidewalks. I don't recall exactly what the task had been. We were given all sorts of menial tasks. It was lunchtime and the truck had brought us back to the dining hall for lunch break. (The Air Force brass had decided that the term mess hall wasn't fitting and had ordered that the facility where troops ate their meals would henceforth be called the dining hall. It didn't matter what the brass said, the enlisted men still called them mess halls.) All but two of us had been ordered off the truck to get in line at the mess hall. So, we started talking. "Where you from?" I asked the other guy. Seattle was his answer.

Before leaving home for the Air Force, I had been dating a pretty Irish girl named Rosemary Sheehan. I thought I was in love then, but I realize now that I didn't have the faintest idea of what love actually was. Anyway, I had a photo of Rosie, as I called her and showed it to the other guy. He pulled out a picture of a pretty young girl and said her name was Vera. We put the photos back in our wallets and began talking of—whatever. It turned out that we both liked country music, and our favorite country music entertainer was Hank Snow, a small man with a big voice, ego and, as I learned years later, a nasty, hateful disposition. The conversation drifted to what we wanted to do when our hitch in the Air Force was finished. My plan was to use the GI Bill, for which I would become eligible upon discharge, to go to a flying school, get the various pilot certificates necessary, and hopefully get a job as an airline pilot. I asked the other guy—his name was Harold Thompson—what he wanted to do, and his answer floored me. He said he wanted to be a hobo and he thought it would be fun to live that life. (I never thought of it at the time, but I later asked Vera if he had invited her to be a hobo along with him. She told me he hadn't.) Harold and I became good friends. We both liked country music and drinking beer.

As fate would have it, or I guess I should say, as the US Air Force would have it, my buddy Harold got orders to South Carolina far from Seattle. I was ordered to Larson Air Force Base, Moses Lake, Washington and 185 miles from Seattle. So begins the tale of how I met my future wife.

Fast forward to Christmas 1952. Harold and I had kept in touch through the mail. I got a letter from Harold saying that he was coming to Seattle for Christmas and that I should join him in Seattle to party and try to drink the town dry. A couple of days before Christmas, I hitchhiked to Seattle and went to Harold's parents' home. Harold hadn't arrived yet. When I explained that Harold and I had become friends they greeted me warmly and apologized that they didn't have anywhere for me to sleep. Harold's older brother Hank, took me to a nearby cheapo hotel and said that he would come and pick me up if Harold arrived. Two days before Christmas, I was awake but still lying in bed, there was a knock on the door. Upon opening the door, I saw it was Harold's older brother, Hank. He said that Harold had arrived and hadn't been told that I had come to Seattle. He had come to take me to their parents' home. As I walked in the door and Harold saw me, a big grin spread across his face. He jumped up from his chair, and we began slapping each other on the back and asking about each other's trip. His trip was much more interesting than mine; he had gotten "hops" on several different military airplanes. My trip was just a couple of different hitchhiking rides in cars.

Well, my hitchhiking trip to Seattle had an interesting beginning. I had caught a ride from Larson Air Force Base into the town of Moses Lake then walked to the west edge of town. I stuck up my thumb. The first car to come along pulled over and stopped; and what a car: a 1952 Cadillac convertible. I trotted alongside, opened the door, and put my little "AWOL bag" behind the front seat. Then, when I glanced over and looked at the driver I was surprised to see—an attractive young woman wearing a fur coat. I had expected to see a middle-aged man in a business suit. "How far you going," I asked. She smiled at me, shrugged her shoulders a couple of times, and giggled, "I don't know." Well, well, well!

At that time, I was not quite eighteen years old. It never occurred to me that she might have an older husband who didn't make her happy or that she was a lady engaged in "the oldest profession." Besides, I was much too shy to try and find out although my hormone generator was "running amok" as young men's do at that age. I got in on the passenger side and began a ride I was probably fortunate to survive. I smoked at that time in my life, and as street-lights of Moses Lake faded away in the rear-view mirror, she offered me a cigarette. I took one. She shook one halfway out of the pack took it between her lips and cooed, "Come on sweetie, give a girl a light." I pushed in the cigarette lighter and when it popped out held it toward her. She took my hand and pressed the glowing tip of the lighter to the cigarette held in her lips. She gave my hand a gentle squeeze. I lit my cigarette and puffed away, not knowing enough to try to start a conversation. Then the Caddie entered fog.

The Columbia Basin often is blanketed by dense fog during the winter months. We were headed west on Highway 10, a two-lane highway the precursor to I-90. She had been driving 60 to 65 before entering the fog, and in the fog she didn't slow down at all. We sped along in silence for a few minutes, then without warning, she floor-boarded it! I watched the speedometer climb to 70, 80, 90 miles per hour through the pea-soup fog. Fortunately, no red tail lights suddenly burst into sight ahead of us. We drove about five minutes at that crazy speed when a road-side sign flashed by warning of an intersection. She jammed on the brakes and slid to a stop in the middle of the intersection. She pointed to the dashboard clock and said in a voice that sounded exasperated, "I have to be back in town for a party in 20 minutes." I thanked her for the ride and got out. She didn't say a word. She wheeled that Caddie around, tires squealing and headed back east, tail lights disappearing into the fog. Whatever she was looking for, a lover or a customer, she apparently decided that this naïve young kid wasn't what she wanted.

The intersection was known as the George Y; continuing west went on to Ellensburg and eventually Seattle. There was hardly any traffic from either direction and no street light. It was so dark that I couldn't see my feet. I wondered how long I would stand there hoping for a ride. Then, a west bound car passed and went out of sight in the fog. A few moments later an east-bound car slowly passed by me then did a U-turn and came to a stop where I was standing. It was a young couple from Ellensburg. They hadn't been able to stop in time to pick me up when they passed me west bound and had made two U-turns just so they could give a ride to this guy standing there in the foggy darkness. I have never forgotten their kindness. They went further out of their way to drop me at the western edge of Ellensburg where I would be more likely to catch a ride.

Back in Seattle following my buddy Harold's arrival, his mother cooked up a huge, hearty, delicious breakfast. We pigged out on bacon, eggs, sausage, pancakes, endless black coffee so strong that a spoon would almost stand up in it, and some Norwegian pastries. I don't remember what they were called; I couldn't spell it anyway. Hank had served in the RAF during World War II. He had been copilot on Short Sunderlands, big, four engine flying boats built by Short Brothers in Northern Ireland. I was fascinated when he recounted tales of flying in those monster airplanes, fifty feet above the water, twisting and turning in and out of Norwegian fjords.

Harold's mother and father were both Norwegian immigrants. They spoke English well but with a strong accent. His father's name was Olaf, called Oly as most Olafs are. His mother's name was Magnhild (I had trouble then pronouncing it; I still do!). Seems like "Maggie" would have been a fitting nickname, but it wasn't used. In addition to his older brother Hank, Harold had an older sister, Margaret, a sister a year or two younger, Esther, and three much younger brothers. Margaret was married to a WWII Navy veteran, Jerry Stocks. Jerry was from El Dorado, Arkansas and so naturally was nicknamed Arkie. Arkie loved country music, dancing and having a bunch of friends and relatives to his house to dance, drink beer and party.

Harold had arrived early in the morning of December 23. I had to report back for duty at 5:00 p.m. on Christmas Day. Whoopee! Two nights of partying comin' up!

Memories of the next two days and nights are blurry at best. Sometime during those two days and nights, Harold introduced me to Vera. It turned out that Vera loved country music and also sang and accompanied herself on the guitar. Harold and Vera's favorite country music entertainer was also mine. He was a Canadian from Nova Scotia by the name of Clarence E. Snow; it must have been Snow's agent who decided that Clarence wasn't a suitable name for a country music performer, so he went by the stage name of Hank Snow. He was a small man with a big voice. Like so many he was a "flash in the pan"; he had about a ten-year run, during the late 1940s through 1950s before his star flamed out.

For two days—December 23 and 24, 1952—it was drink beer, eat, play music, dance, sleep/pass out and repeat. Sometime during those two days and nights I met Harold's older sister Margaret and her husband Arkie. Somehow, we all learned that my birthday, March 11, was the same as Margaret's, and that I should plan to come back to Seattle for a big birthday party. I planned to do so; I didn't need coaxing. On Christmas morning I awoke with a big headache and realized that I had to head back to Moses Lake to report for duty at five in the afternoon. Harold drove me to the west shore of Lake Washington on what was then Highway 10—I-90 didn't exist until years later—to hitchhike to the base at Moses Lake. Back then, for anyone dressed in uniform, catching a ride was easy, and I made it in time for duty.

Time passed. My birthday was approaching, and I was able to get my duty scheduled so I could go to Seattle for the big birthday party at Margaret and Arkie's house. And it was at Arkie's that I met Vera's younger sister, Violet. It was early evening. The party hadn't really begin to warm up. When I walked in the door there sat a pretty young gal, playing and singing while accompanying herself on the guitar. At first, I thought it was Vera but she didn't seem to look like I remembered her, but then, I was bleary-eyed most of the Christmas visit. I asked Arkie, "Is that Vera?" Arkie replied, "No. That's her younger sister Violet." As it turned out, there were three sisters, Vera, Violet and Velma, who were only about one year apart in age. They spent their childhood years on a farm in south-central Missouri. The nearby town was called Mountain View. Why? I haven't the faintest idea. There wasn't a mountain in sight; well, not what Washingtonians or even I, who spent his childhood in the Adirondack Mountains of up-state New York state, would call a mountain. Vera, Violet, Velma; families named their children like that down there in rural Missouri. Vera's mother was Velma, her aunts Alma, Thelma and Flora; her uncles, Ellis, Elmus and Elvis.

So, I began seeing Violet. I hadn't even thought of dating Vera; she was my buddy Harold's girl, I wasn't about to try and cut in. My Air Force buddy and roomie at Larson Air Force Base, Carl J. Bottomley who went by his middle-name, Jack, was a hillbilly from a tiny town in West Virginia, I had put together a country music band with several guys from the base. We even had one guy who acted as manager. He had a gift of gab and was able to book us jobs on weekend evenings. The band fell apart after a couple of months. I saved enough money between my military pay and band earnings to buy a beater car: a 1941, two-door fastback Buick. Whenever Jack and I didn't have weekend duty we would head for Seattle. I was dating Violet. Jack was dating Vera's youngest sister, Velma. Violet, I soon learned, was one who liked to play games. She would say that she didn't want to see me anymore then change her mind. Once after she "broke up" with me, Jack and I went on a double date to a drive-in movie. Jack dated Velma, I took Harold's sister, Esther. When we got back to drop Velma at her parents' home, (all three sisters were living with their parents), Violet came storming out and proceeded to throw a fit because I was with Esther. Shame on me! I had Jack take Esther home: in effect dumping her for Violet. I still feel badly about doing that. Esther was a nice young lady.

Then late in the summer of 1953, Harold came to Seattle, and I met him somewhere, somehow during that visit. Aside from recalling that it involved more beer, I don't remember much of that visit except for riding around his neighborhood in southwest Seattle. He was driving somewhat crazy and seemed to be in a rotten mood. I finally coaxed from him what the problem was. He said that Vera had broken up with him. I don't recall anything else about that visit. A short time later I came to Seattle again. Violet was again playing her "I don't want to see you again" game, so Vera and I went out on a date. Same old thing. When I brought Vera home, there came Violet, throwing a fit both at me and Vera. Vera had also been seeing a Coast Guard guy she had met through her cousin, who also was in the Coast Guard. He also played the guitar; music seemed to draw us all together.

Then, I received orders that would send me to Alaska for two years. I was granted thirty days' leave and went back to see parents and friends before I was Alaska bound. Violet and I wrote back and forth a few times; then, in January 1954, I got my final "Dear John" from Violet. Violet was marrying the Coast Guard guy that Vera had been dating. Vera and I began writing to each other, and through letters developed a romance. July 1954. I was granted thirty days' leave and made my way to Seattle. Vera and I were married by a Justice of the Peace on July 17.

We hardly knew each other then, yet here we are over sixty-four years later. It's worked out way better than many of those who were married in a fancy, expensive church wedding.

Dwight age 19

Vera age 21

Cutting Our Wedding Cake 1954

*Dwight and Vera
64 years later*

Chapter 9
Making a Living

Sometimes my parents would give me advice to steer me into the career they thought suitable and say, "If you will only do _____, you will be glad you did." I kinda/sorta did what they wanted. I gave up on my dream of becoming an airline pilot and half-heartedly attempted to follow a career path they approved. But now I'm not glad that I did. My four years in the Air Force were a huge disappointment. I wanted to work on airplanes, but the Air Force ordered me into a job in communications, which didn't much interest me.

After my four-year hitch in the Air Force, I was hired on at Boeing as an assembly mechanic, the absolute bottom of job classifications. I was a high school dropout with only a GED high-school equivalency certificate. I crawled around inside the wings of the B-52, drilling holes, bucking rivets and installing parts. I had GI Bill benefits that I used for college. I enrolled in a night school trigonometry course at the University of Washington, applied myself and earned an A. I guess the A grade in trig convinced the admissions person interviewing me to admit me to the university on a probationary basis.

I found I could handle college okay, but my heart was never in it; I still was trying to create a career that would please my parents. I never completed a bachelor's degree; I accumulated just over half of the credits necessary to graduate. I moved up the ladder at Boeing. I worked hard, but not because I loved my job. I simply wanted to earn more money, so my family and I could afford to partake in the activities that we enjoyed. Within two years I was moved into performing engineering work. After ten years at Boeing, the college courses that I had completed toward a degree in electrical engineering, combined with the engineering work experience I gained at Boeing, qualified me to write the Washington State examination to become licensed as a Professional Electrical Engineer. I passed it!

The state issues an impressive license certificate to those who meet the requirements and pass the written, two-day examination. The day my certificate arrived, my parents and Vera's parents were all at our home. I went to our mailbox and brought in the mail, which happened to include the professional engineer certificate. As I opened the envelope, my father stepped beside me, pulled the certificate from my hands, and proceeded to read aloud the flowery words proclaiming me a Licensed Electrical Engineer. The buttons were popping off his shirt in pride, but his reading it embarrassed me. I finally had done something that made them proud of me. It was an accomplishment that pleased me too. I felt honored that the board reviewing the summation of my work experience considered me qualified enough to take the examination.

Having received a passing grade, I became a member of the engineering profession. I gave up my dream of becoming an airline pilot, but even now I'm not "glad that I did" as I was told many times that I would be. I don't expect that I ever will be. My parents' refusal to support my dream of flying has left me with what feels like a hole in my life. If they had only encouraged me to find the career that I wanted, instead of giving up on my dream, I would have the satisfaction of looking back on my life and knowing that my mom and dad helped me to attain that goal. It also bothers me somewhat to feel that I was a disappointment to them; but I know that it was their problem, not mine. I certainly always had the basics of a comfortable life: food, clothing and shelter. They also did much right by setting good examples of the importance of honesty and kindness to others.

I did get the chance to fly airplanes, small singles and twins, but never came anywhere near becoming a pilot for a major airline. I started quite young, seventeen years old. In early 1953 when I was an enlisted man in the United States Air Force and stationed at Larson Air Force Base, Moses Lake, Washington, I used to telephone home regularly. During one of those calls, after small talk with both parents, I told my father that I was going to take flying lessons at the civilian airport in

Ephrata, Washington. Because my parents helped pay both my sisters' way through college, I assumed that they would help me financially with the cost of learning to fly. When I told my father what I planned to do, what I heard instead of encouragement was a disgusted response: "Oh, all right." Although they never uttered a word of encouragement, they did contribute some money. It seemed to me at the time that they could have done more to help me, but then I had no idea that my parents were running out of my mother's inheritance.

I completed the first step of pilot certificates, successfully passing the written, oral tests and Private Pilot Checkride in September 1953. By 1958 I was four years married and working for Boeing. My father came to Seattle on business and for a visit with me and my family. During his visit, I mentioned that I still hoped to become an airline pilot. Upon hearing that, my father said, "I talked with Eddie Rickenbacker [who then was the president of Eastern Airlines], and he told me that only if a person had been a pilot in the military would an airline hire them." I now think that my father made up that story, and it makes me furious to think that he deliberately lied to me.

After hearing the Eddie Rickenbacker story from my father, I finally gave up on my dream of a flying career. I flew hardly at all until 1977 when I bought an airplane, leased it to a flying club, and paid the expense of ownership by doing aerial photographs. I began flying again. I applied myself to earning more pilot certificates and ratings: commercial, instrument, multi-engine, flight instructor, and airline transport. Finally, after retiring from a job with a company where I had worked for twenty-one years, I was hired as a pilot for a small air freight and charter company. I was sixty-five years of age, and for the first time I was actually getting paid, though not much, to fly airplanes. Not until then did I realize how much I loved flying. I became furious about what my parents had done to prevent me from pursuing my dream. They had their own ideas of what I should do with my life.

Part II

Lessons

Chapter 10
Compassion

I'm far from being Mother Teresa; however, I feel there are small things that anyone can do that will contribute in some tiny way to make the world a better, kinder place for all. What I learned somewhere during my long life and try to do every time I interact with another person is to say or do something that may lift them up, like a compliment on some aspect of their appearance—tell them they have a friendly or beautiful smile—or if I can't think of anything to say, I just give a friendly smile and wish them a good day. Sometimes I fail.

At times the connection I feel to someone I've just met is so strong that the emotions are almost overwhelming. Once, half a lifetime ago, I was concluding a discussion with a buyer for a company with which I had been working for several months. The other people involved in the meeting had left the room. I enjoy people and having a job in engineering sales gave me the opportunity to meet many people. I usually asked them about details of their lives: their families, their plans, their ambitions. In a previous lunch meeting with the buyer, I had asked about his family, and he told me that he and his wife had two little girls and that one of them was undergoing treatment for cancer.

During the time before our next meeting I thought often of the heartache and worry that the buyer and his wife were experiencing. My two youngest boys were close to the age of their girls. The thought of anything happening to any of my children tore at my heart. Somehow the memory of my blurting out the word God came to mind. As years had passed, I tried to figure out what God was like, and if He, She, or It existed. At that time of my life I had come to call God "the Big Boss" when I thought of God. I had heard about people praying to God, but I couldn't honestly say that I believed God would do what people asked for in their prayers. But I couldn't imagine that this God entity would be upset with me if I sent off a thought-prayer for the buyer's little girl.

I figured, well—maybe it would help. So, I asked the Big Boss to cure the little girl.

When the next meeting with the customer concluded, I waited in the buyer's office until just the two of us remained, the buyer and me. I offered my hand, and he clasped mine. As my eyes welled up with tears, I choked up but managed to say, "I put some words in with the Big Boss for your little girl, I hope it helps." Tears filled his eyes as he squeezed my hand more firmly, and he said in a voice that was almost a whisper, "Thank you." I never knew the outcome of this human story. That was the last time I ever saw the buyer; he left the company.

Another encounter that occurred years ago has always stuck in my memory. I was in a fast food restaurant, had placed my order and was waiting for it to be prepared. A black man was also waiting, and I couldn't help but notice his appearance: smooth-shaven but for a well-trimmed mustache, neat haircut showing below a smart cap, handsome jacket, white shirt and tie, sharply creased trousers, shoes that were shined to a gleaming polish. I went over to him and said, "Sir, I would like to compliment you on your appearance, you really look sharp!" He smiled, thanked me, we shook hands and he said, "You should see my cab; it is kept the same way—and I do very well in the tips department." I told him that I was not surprised.

All my life, from childhood, I never could understand why people were prejudiced against another person or persons because of their nationality, race or religion. It must be in my genes because there were subtle whisperings in my household about somebody being Jewish, Catholic, Negro, Irish—anything other than what the family was. I never heard anything that suggested violence against any group; it was just like an air of " Well they shouldn't be discriminated against, but we're better than they are." I never could understand that. I either liked someone because they were friendly with me, or I avoided them—not because of what they were but just because they didn't seem to like me. I never felt that I was "better than" anyone else of a different race, ethnicity or religion. But I also was told that my father's family home in Franklin, Ohio, had been a stop on the Underground Railroad which helped escaped slaves reach safety in Canada. On that same side of the family, my great-uncle Wilbur Paterson Thirkield was president of Howard University from 1906 through 1912. The science building is dedicated to his honor; and I was told, he did much to better the lives of black people.

When I enlisted in the United States Air Force one day after my seventeenth birthday in 1952 and less than four years after the military was integrated, there was still a lot of prejudice against blacks. I remember a discussion with a guy from Georgia. I said I didn't think it was right that blacks had to sit at the back of the bus. His response was, "You would if you lived there. They all stink!" I wasn't quick enough to respond with, "What about white people that stink? Shouldn't they have to sit in the back of the bus?" I sometimes hung around with some of the blacks, and I was quite certain that the white guys from the south didn't like me doing it.

Over time I learned of the terrible ways blacks were treated in the Jim Crow South. It made me sick then and still does to know of the horrible abuses that blacks suffered, including lynchings, beatings, and torture. It is a sad chapter of man's inhumanity to man—and it still goes on—but back to the impeccably dressed cab owner. I said to him, "I want you to know that I'm sickened by what white people did to blacks." His response surprised me. He said, "Well, I appreciate you saying that." Then he added, "At least they didn't try to exterminate us like they did the Jews."

I have long remembered this brief meeting. I hope that my words of apology, as I guess they were, did some small good. If everyone would just do little, kind gestures it would help us all to live in greater harmony.

Another time I reached out to someone in obvious pain was a week after the terrorist attacks of September 11, 2001, when fear and paranoia of all things Islamic and Middle Eastern reigned. On Monday, September

10th, I had flown a route from Seattle, Boeing Field to Portland, Oregon to Boise, Idaho, then made a deadhead (no freight) return to Boeing Field. If I had been flying that route the next day, I would have been ordered to land at the nearest suitable airport, which would probably have been the one in a small town called John Day in the wilds of eastern Oregon.

Aviation in the United States was in chaos all of the day on September 11th. By the next day the major airlines were getting back into their schedules but the mini-airlines like the one for which I was a pilot, weren't back into regular operation until the week of September 17. On Tuesday, September 18, I flew a route that stopped at Yakima, Washington in the early evening. The courier delivering the freight I had to pick up was delayed, so I walked to the airport terminal and sat down in a waiting area.

When I got up to leave and turned around, I saw a gentleman wearing a turban, seeming to stare at the wall not far in front of him, with a faraway, dejected expression. It occurred to me that some hate-filled person had unloaded a barrage of cruel words, probably accusing him of being joyful about the destruction of the World Trade Center.

I walked over to him and said, "Sir," and paused. When he raised his eyes to meet mine, I said, "I believe that most of you people who wear turbans just want to live in peace." I offered my hand and he responded by extending his. We shook hands for a moment, his eyes welled with tears as did mine, and he said almost in a whisper, "Thank you so much." As I turned to leave, my gaze met that of an older lady sitting nearby who had witnessed and probably overheard my encounter with the turbaned man; there were tears in her eyes and she nodded to me with an expression that told me she thought I had done something worthwhile. I am so glad that I made that gesture of the brotherhood of all people. I hope that it has rippled out through the world to help bring understanding and peace on earth.

And then there was the time I came across a story in a newspaper about a young couple who had lost a child to illness. Their child's death was only a few days earlier. Reading their story brought back memories of the anguish Vera and I suffered soon after losing our son twenty-seven years before. When we would do the mundane things necessary to go on living, we would see the rest of the world going on as though nothing had happened, and it seemed as though no one else cared what we were going through. The couple lived in a small town nearby. I found a telephone book and looked up the couple's names and found what I thought was their number. I mentally went back and forth, wondering if I should call their number and, if someone answered, what to say.

After probably ten or fifteen minutes of pondering, I called the number. A female voice answered. I asked if she and her husband were the couple who had lost their child. When she said yes, I told her that I was someone who had lost a child and that I had called to let her know that there was another person in the world who "knows how you feel." I said something like, "I hope my call will in some small way help to ease the pain you and your husband are suffering."

We talked for maybe fifteen or twenty minutes. We wept together over the telephone. I told her that the pain would lessen, that I hadn't "gotten over it after twenty-seven years but that it gets 'easier.'" After a while, we seemed to be talked out, the tears had stopped flowing. She thanked me for calling and said that it did help to know that someone else knows how they feel and cares.

Reaching out to perfect strangers is not easy because you never know how the person will react. Will they appreciate your concern or your sympathy, or will they resent it? There's some risk involved with showing others that you care. I'm always willing to take that risk.

Chapter 11
Death of Our Son-
God's Punishment?

My wife, Vera and I sat on either side of our sixteen-year-old son, Kenneth. We watched Ken's heartbeat on the monitor as it faded away until there was none. We had lost our precious son.

At the time of this writing more than thirty-eight years have passed, but not a day goes by that I don't live again in memory the tragedy that befell my wife Vera and me in April 1979. I'm not crippled by it. I don't cry about it daily. I don't cry about it very often after all these years. Only now and then, when something triggers whatever it is that pushes me over the edge into the abyss of never-ending heartache, do I break down into sobs and tears. Those spells don't last long, probably not more than one or two minutes. Writing this will cause the tears to flow and that's okay. I'm not ashamed that I break down occasionally; after all,

Number One Son, Wes, wife Cindy and grandkids,
Jon, Dan and Kira

aren't tears a tribute to that which one has lost?

Vera and I had nearly abandoned hope that we would have children together. We had been married for eight years and pregnancy just didn't happen. We had the son who had been born to Vera and a young man to whom she had been married for only a little more than three years. It was almost a childhood marriage; she was eighteen and he was nineteen. He wasn't a bad guy; he was just a kid who didn't seem to accept the responsibility of marriage. One day he came home and announced that he had enlisted in the Air Force. Off he went to the Air Force, and Vera moved back in with her parents, feeling that the marriage wasn't going to work. She got a divorce about a year later. Wesley was not quite three when Vera and I were married. I had adopted him as quickly as it could be accomplished after his father asked if I would want to.

Miracles sometimes happen. Vera and I had two sons together, Kenneth Lee, born February 28, 1963 and Timothy John, born May 14, 1965. Wesley, which we always shortened to Wes, was a wonderful great-big-brother. He would give them piggy-back rides, read to his little brothers, and push them around the hallway in a little cardboard box with wheels on it as fast as he could, until they laughed so hard that tears

Son Tim age 18   *Son Ken age 16*

were running down their cheeks.

I was in the delivery room with Vera when both Kenny and Tim came into this world. I think the doctor and nurses of the delivery team were more worried about me than about Vera. The miracle of birth overwhelmed me then, and even now as I relive those moments, my eyes fill with tears. Seeing those tiny human beings emerge into the world all wet, seeing their little chests expand for the first breath, and hearing them cry filled me with emotions that I can't begin to describe. After I was chased from the delivery room, I went outside, curled into a sitting fetal position leaning against the wall, and sobbed, certainly not from sadness but from a mixture of joy and the wonder of it all. A nurse checked on me to see if I was okay.

Throughout elementary and junior high school Kenneth, or Kenny, as we usually called him had been a star; he was not a super star, but he had done well. He had a gift for music. He had begun trumpet lessons during elementary school and been in band in both elementary and junior high school. We had enrolled him in private lessons, and his instructor told us that he was among the best of his students. Kenny and another boy bounced back and forth for first and second trumpet chair in junior high band.

We couldn't understand what went wrong when Kenny started high school. He somehow got on the wrong track. His circle of friends changed to the group on the fringe. He got into a fight with another boy and broke the boy's nose. That caused his expulsion from the regular high school and into an alternative school program for kids who couldn't get along. His problems caused us much loss of sleep.

Kenny turned sixteen in 1979 and, of course, one of the most important events in his life was getting his driver's license. I should have realized that he wasn't responsible enough to drive, but it's so easy to do the shoulda-coulda-woulda routine. Monday morning quarterbacking is another term. I'm sure that anyone who has a supremely important event go terribly wrong has beaten themselves up over what they did wrong. I know I'll continue to do it for as long as I live.

April 1979, I was in Spokane, Washington on a business trip. It was about nine o'clock in the evening. I was in the bar of the hotel where I was staying, nursing a beer and listening to a band I thought was pretty good. I was almost the only one sitting at the bar. The bartender took a phone call, turned to me, asked my name, and then handed me the phone. It was Vera, and her voice was shaking as she told me that Kenny had been involved in an automobile accident. I asked, "How bad?" and she said that she didn't know for certain, but it sounded like it was "pretty bad." He had been transported to the trauma unit of Seattle Harborview hospital.

I went to my room and called the hospital to see if I could learn more about Kenny's condition. After a long delay, a neurologist came on. He said he had "reduced" the fracture. I asked if Kenny was paralyzed. He said, "Yes." I asked if the paralysis was permanent, and he said they wouldn't know for a couple of days.

I hurriedly packed, checked out of the motel and began the three-hundred-mile drive to Seattle. I was worried that I might not be able to buy gas. An oil crisis was winding down. Fortunately, I was able to fill up at a small town about fifty miles west of Spokane, which would be enough to get to Seattle. I drove and I worried. I drove and I worried. I arrived at the hospital at about four-thirty in the morning and found my way to the trauma center. Vera was there with her mother and our oldest son, Wes, and his wife, Cindy. Vera was at Kenny's bedside near his head. I rushed to her, and we clung to each other sobbing. Ken was totally conscious but couldn't speak. Because of the paralysis he couldn't breathe. A ventilator had been inserted through an incision into his trachea. He could do no more than shake his head yes or no and raise his arms, but he could not move hands, or legs or his feet. He looked at me and our eyes met. He formed words with his lips and face. He would form a word, then I would say what I thought it was. He would shake his head yes or no. By working back and forth this way, he finally got across the words, "I really screwed up."

I told him, "You sure did, Son, but your mom and I love you just as much as ever."

We stayed at the hospital for hours. We would be at his bedside until a nurse would ask us to leave so they could attend to him. We would go to a waiting room where there were other people who were there because of injured loved ones. In the bed next to Kenny was a teenage girl who had also been injured in an auto accident. She was in a coma. I have always wondered if she recovered. I hope she did.

We all were exhausted having been awake for over twenty-four hours. I recall trying to sleep but don't believe I did. I don't think any of us slept. I remember trying to pray, but I was so tired after being awake for more than thirty hours that I was unable to concentrate. In spite of the emotional turmoil, the body continues with its normal functions. We would get hungry, go to the cafeteria, but be unable to choke down more than a few nibbles. Then we would feel guilty about taking care of normal activities because it seemed like all normal activities should stop. How could life ever be normal again?

The accident happened on Wednesday evening. On Thursday evening at about nine o'clock, a neurologist came to Kenny's bed to look in on him. He took a small instrument from his pocket that looked like a miniature hand cultivator. He began scratching Kenny with the instrument beginning at his feet while asking if Kenny could feel the scratching. Vera and I watched with our hearts in our throats. When the doctor had finished, he turned to us and led us only a few steps away to the end of the ward. He told us then that Kenny would not recover; he would remain a quadriplegic for as long as he might live. When he said this, it might have been possible for Kenny to hear. Vera and I clung to each other and sobbed uncontrollably. Why, I wonder, didn't that doctor didn't take us to some secluded location?

Vera and I were so wrung out that we went home and actually slept. We weren't told that the nurses could set up a cot by Kenny's bedside, or

I would have taken Vera home and returned to the hospital to be close to him. I still feel guilty that I left him alone for Thursday and Friday nights.

When we came to see Kenny Friday morning, he had been placed in a setup called a Stryker frame, and he had a metal "halo" attached to his head. This was done so that his neck injury, fractures to cervical vertebrae C3 and C4, would be kept in traction. The Stryker Frame also rotated such that he would not be lying on either his back or front side long enough to cause bed sores. When we arrived, the frame was turned so that Kenny was facing the floor. What a heartbreaking situation for a sixteen-year-old to find himself experiencing. We had been skiing less than two months before.

Friday passed by. Kenny would be rotated. We would talk to him and tell him not to give up. We called friends to tell them of the accident and of Kenny's dreadful prognosis for recovery. People came; people went. I had called my sisters, Lueza, who lived in New York City, and Mary Belle, who lived in Brownsville, Texas. My mother was living with Lueza and her family. Vera and I still were numb because of the emotional trauma. It seemed as if time stood still, and yet it passed, and again it was late night.

Late that evening while Kenny was still wide awake and facing the ceiling, I scratched the sole of one of his feet with my fingernail. A doctor had shown me a test that was performed to determine if there were any "messages" reaching the feet from the brain. The response was called the Babinski reflex. If the toes curl up when the sole of the foot is stroked, it means that there is damage to the spinal cord. I stroked the sole of his foot. It seemed to me that the toes didn't curl up! I asked Kenny to move his legs—and it seemed to me that he did! I burst into tears of joy. I thought he would get well. Vera and I went home again feeling that there was hope for Kenny's recovery. We left when Kenny was sleeping.

Saturday morning, back at the hospital. Kenny couldn't move his legs. I must have wanted to see movement so desperately that I thought I had. A different neurologist appeared. He led Vera and me to a nearby room. He told us that Kenny would not recover from his paralysis and would have to live with a respirator to help him breathe. He couldn't move anything from his shoulders down to his feet. The doctor asked what we wanted them to do. He said that Kenny could be kept alive hooked up to a machine, but that he would develop pneumonia. The pneumonia could be cured with antibiotics, but it would recur again and again until finally it would result in his death. The doctor said that Kenny might be able to breathe enough without the respirator to survive for a few days, but possibly for no more than a few hours.

After Vera and I had recovered somewhat from this devastating news, we decided that Kenny had to be the one to make the decision. How would it be right for us to decide that he would have to live as a quadriplegic? Then again, how would it be right for us to remove him from life support? Vera was so grief-stricken that she was almost unable to speak, so I told her that I would go to Kenny and let him make the life or death decision himself.

The doctor and I went to Kenny's Stryker Frame. Kenny was facing up. The doctor began to describe the prognosis, but he was using medical terms that I thought Kenny wouldn't understand. Between sobs, I interrupted and said, "What he's saying, Kenny, is that you won't recover from this paralysis. You will be in this condition for as long as you live. What do you want to happen?" Without hesitation Kenny began forming words with his lips. I spoke aloud what I thought he was saying, and he would nod his head if what I said was what he was wanting to say. He formed the words, "I. Want. To. Die." And as I stood there, tears streaming down my cheeks and sobbing, he began forming more words. The nurse standing by interpreted: "Put – my – arms – around – my - dad." As I bent over him, the nurse put his limp arms around me, and I choked out the words: "It's okay, Kenny. I wouldn't want to live either with what you are facing." After a few moments, I told Kenny that I would go tell his mom of his decision. He nodded, and I guessed it was an "okay." I left his bedside to tell Vera, and after more holding each other and seemingly endless tears, we went back to his bedside. Vera bent over him, and a nurse put Kenny's arms around her. Then Vera told him that she understood and supported him in his decision.

We phoned people to let them know of Kenny's decision. We called Vera's sisters—Velma lived on Guam, Violet in Michigan—as well as my mother and sisters Lueza and Mary Belle. Friends in the local area, coworkers and others from my office either called or came by the hospital to offer what support they could. Two adults who were parents of friends of Kenny or Tim were among those who offered the most comfort, probably because they had children of near the same age and could understand the agony we were experiencing.

We floated through Saturday as if in a terrible nightmare from which we couldn't wake up. People came and went. The respirator was removed, and Kenny continued to breathe unassisted: shallowly but enough to sustain him. He was totally conscious, and we could communicate. We talked about dying. He said he was not afraid to die

Evening came. A nurse gave Kenny a hypo to help him sleep. While he slept we went to the cafeteria. When we returned Kenny was awake and still breathing. We talked more. I said to him, "Maybe you'll fool everyone and walk out of here." Kenny grinned. I asked Kenny how we should handle funeral arrangements. He said, "The cheapest way." I asked if cremation was okay, and he nodded yes. I asked what we should do with his ashes. He had gotten very involved in bike racing on a dirt track with lots of curves, bumps, humps, and jumps. He asked me to spread his ashes on a bike track where he had raced. As I didn't think that might be allowed, I asked if I could scatter them from an airplane above the summit of Mount Rainier, so I would think of him whenever I happened to see it. He agreed. I told him that he would have a really gigantic monument. He grinned. I asked him if we could donate any of his body parts, which would benefit the living. He immediately agreed that we should do so.

We found out later that his corneas went to the Lions Eye Bank and his skin to the burn center. We were told that his kidneys couldn't be used as transplants. I was not told why his kidneys couldn't be used, but I still don't understand why. We wanted any possible good to come from this tragedy. I wonder if I have ever looked into someone's eyes that were saved from blindness because of Kenny's corneas. I have thoughts, probably crazy, that his kidneys were harvested and surreptitiously sold to pay off some doctor's student loans.

Later in the evening, a nurse came to tell us that a Catholic priest had come to baptize Kenny and give him last rites. As we were not Catholic or associated with any denomination, we had not had Kenny baptized. My sister Mary Belle had converted to Catholicism and was very devout, and she had taken it upon herself to do what she thought had to be done. It irritated me that she had forced her beliefs upon us, but I thought if it made her feel better, it couldn't do any harm. Vera was quite angry about it but didn't want to cause a big fuss. So, the priest went through the rituals and left. Kenny was given another hypo to make him sleep again. Kenny slept. We sat on either side of the Stryker Frame bed and fitfully dozed.

Around midnight we woke. Seeing that Kenny had awakened, I asked him to move his legs. There was no motion. Another hypo. Kenny drifted off. We sat beside him, with Vera on one side and I on the other. We held his hand and stroked his arms. We would occasionally glance at the heart monitor. It had been regular, then as both of us happened to be watching, the waveform changed shape and suddenly stopped! I softly said to Vera, "Kenny's gone." Vera made a sound like I will never forget. I can only describe that sound as something between a moan and a muffled low scream, not loud, but loud enough that a nurse came immediately. Vera was on her feet, bending over Kenny, kissing his face, caressing his cheeks. I sat holding his right hand in mine, sobbing softly. It seemed strange, but his heartbeat began again, the monitor beeping. It kept on beating regularly, not slowing, but the strength of each heartbeat slowly ebbed. We stayed there beside him, touching his skin, caressing his arms and face until there was no more trace of his heartbeat. Our precious, beloved son Kenneth Lee Thirkield had died. After a while, we left Kenny's lifeless body on the Stryker frame bed. We went home, fell into bed, and slept from physical and mental exhaustion and heartbreak.

Later in the morning, almost immediately after awakening and getting out of bed, a wave of unbearable grief overcame me. I collapsed to the bedroom floor and curled into a fetal position, rocking back and forth, screaming and sobbing, "Kenny's gone! Kenny's gone! Kenny's gone!" Vera held me and comforted me as best she could. My breakdown didn't last long, but I still break down occasionally, after so many years.

We wondered what to do for some sort of a memorial service since we had not been members of a church. At that time in our lives we didn't have a well-defined mental image of a Supreme Being. We weren't certain there was one, but I still had to wonder if God had caused Kenny to be in this accident. Was this my punishment for being uncertain of God existence? Somehow, I couldn't believe that. If a God exists, it would not do that.

Our family had loved the outdoors. We had camped, hiked, skied, and taken San Juan Island cruises on a boat I had built in our backyard. We decided, therefore, to have a memorial gathering for Kenny in a natural setting, a small, mostly unimproved public park. It had crude bench seats and was situated among tall fir and cedar trees. We had a friend who was an attorney and a very good speaker, so I asked him if he could compose something appropriate. He agreed to say a few words.

Relatives arrived. Vera's sister, Violet, came from Michigan. My sister Lueza and my mother came from New York City. Vera's mother lived nearby, as did our son Wes and his wife. Our youngest son, Tim, was not quite fourteen and, of course, still living with us. There was a lot to do—people to pick up at the airport, telephone calls to make, and neighbors wanting to stop by with hugs and food or sometimes tears.

84

The mothers of two of our sons' friends were the most caring, yet before Kenny's death we barely had known them. Other people with whom we had been much closer disappeared.

The memorial service and gathering turned out to be beautiful in an unexpected way. Vera and I and our family members were there, and our attorney friend said appropriate words. Just the school year before, Kenny's last year of junior high school, he had one of the leading roles in a musical production. The theater production had been written and musically scored by a husband and wife duo who taught at Kenny's school. They came to Kenny's memorial. After the attorney's eulogy, the male teacher stepped to the front and spoke beautiful, touching words about Kenny that brought many people who were there to tears. Then as the ceremony ended, we got up and turned to leave. We were astonished to see the number of people there. It seemed most of Kenny's sophomore class had come. It brought me to tears to see how many people, young adults, and parents that Kenny's existence had touched during his sixteen years, one month and nineteen days of life.

The week following Kenny's death went by quickly. There were many things to get done. Following the memorial in the forest, we had a reception at our home for friends, relatives and neighbors. Neighbors that we were not actually acquainted with, beyond a friendly wave and nod, stopped in to offer their sympathies. After all the relatives from far away had been dropped off at the airport, there was a myriad of other details to attend to.

Finally, our lives had to return to "normal," though we felt we would never be normal again. I have heard that some people never resume anything like the life they lived before the death of a child. We would perform the mundane activities that everyday living required though we were smothering in a blanket of grief. We did what we had to do because there was no other choice. We had to keep on going because of our youngest son, Tim. I went back to work. Vera was not working outside the home, so she had to bear her grief alone when I was at work.

One day I got home from work, and Vera was fixing dinner. Tim was gone somewhere with friends. Vera had been going through Kenny's bedroom that day. As I walked into the kitchen, she turned to me and almost collapsed in my arms. She sobbed out the words, "I don't think I'll ever be happy again." We held onto each other until the tears slowed and stopped.

Then the funeral home called to tell us that we could pick up Kenny's ashes. I was a qualified pilot of small, single-engine airplanes and made arrangements to use an airplane for the flight over Mount Rainier to scatter his ashes. Our oldest son, Wes, asked to go with me. It was a day with a low overcast, and at that time I was not certificated to fly on instruments, so I had to hope I could find a hole in the overcast that I could climb through to ascend to the clear blue sky above. As luck would have it, I was able to find a big hole and climb into the clear blue sky. Mount Rainier appeared in all its snow-covered majesty. We had a portable oxygen bottle that kept us alert and legal. It was not a high-performance single, so it took about a half hour to climb to 15,500 feet, above the summit of Mount Rainier which is 14,411 feet. I probably climbed slower than I could have because scattering Kenny's ashes seemed like closing the book on his life. I circled three times around the summit, and then

Mt. Rainier, Washington. Son Kenny's Monument

I opened the side window and let Kenny's ashes go into the slip-stream of rarefied air as I sobbed and tears flooded my cheeks. Vera and I hope that Kenny's ashes have found their way through nature's processes to a place below the summit where they may have provided nourishment to help something beautiful grow—an alpine flower, lush green sword fern, or maybe a beautiful, tall Douglas fir that will long outlive Vera and me.

I can't speak for Vera's feelings. I know that she suffered grief then and still does, but she keeps her feelings pretty much locked inside. That's her way of coping. Me? For two to three years I had a tightness or discomfort or ache in my gut. Little by little it decreased before finally, the physical ache was gone. To anyone who may read this who has lost a child, I can tell you from having lived through it that it will become easier to live with your tragedy. I doubt if you ever will "get over it" nor do I want to; it would be like forgetting him. It's been many years for us at the time of this writing. I have shed many tears as I wrote this. I don't ever want to get over it because that would be like Kenny never existed. Any tears that I shed I consider to be a tribute to his memory.

To anyone who has not lost a child but encounters, knows of, or is close to someone who has, this is what not to do: Don't ever say to them, "I know how you feel." You can't possibly know how they feel. Do be there for them. Don't disappear because you're afraid you might break down in tears. If you do break down, it's okay. If you can hug them as you cry, that shows them that your heart aches for them. Just don't run away and hide.

A week or so after I had returned to work, I was in a discussion with a customer seated behind his desk. All the people that I interfaced with in the course of my job had heard of the death of my son. My grief must have been apparent, for the individual behind the desk looked up and asked, "When are you going to snap out of it?" I felt like jumping over his desk and punching him out!

Toward the completion of writing this memoir, I came across

this Hopi Prayer. It had appeared years earlier in the Seattle Times newspaper. A young Hopi woman soldier had been killed in one of the Iraq wars and the prayer had been read at her funeral service held in Tuba City, Arizona. The words are so touching to me; it is almost as though Kenny is speaking to me. Reading the words brings me to tears but also somehow, someway, it is comforting.

Hopi Prayer

Do not stand at my grave and weep
I am not there
I do not sleep
I am a thousand winds that blow
I am the diamond glint on snow
I am the sunlight on ripened grain
I am the gentle autumn's rain
When you awake in the morning's hush
I am the swift uplifting rush
Of quiet birds in circling flight
I am the soft shining stars at night
Do not stand at my grave and cry
I am not there
I did not die

Kenneth Lee Thirkield
28 February, 1963–19 April, 1979

Chapter 12
First Conversation with Old One

I finally did get a job flying airplanes though it wasn't until I was sixty-five years old, and how I got there is another story. I began flying as a pilot for a small air freight company that flew out of Boeing Field, Seattle, Washington.

Mini-airline Aeroflight Pilots 2009 – My pilot job employer Owner
Michael Hill standing left
Me front row left

Cessna 421 My favorite airplane

Piper Chieftain My
2nd favorite airplane

This flying job made for much time that I had to amuse myself. The most common routine was to fly somewhere in the morning. The flight might take as little as forty-five minutes or as long as two and a half hours. Then, I had to unload the freight, have the airplane fueled, and do a check of the airplane to be sure that no maintenance was required, such that the airplane would be "okay to go" for the return flight in the evening. Usually all activities were taken care of between nine and ten in the morning. The return flight would depart between six and nine in the evening. The company provided a car to get around and a place called a "crash pad" to catch up on sleep or otherwise occupy idle time.

I really enjoyed the free time. There were many things I would do to pass the day. Most of the time, I'd need to catch two or three hours of sleep because with the split-up time it was only possible to sleep four or five hours when I finally got home in the evening. I have always loved to read, so I usually brought a book along to read. Sometimes I'd hang out in a library or browse in a bookstore. I had an old beater guitar that I'd always take along and sometimes I'd plunk awhile on it, or I'd go to a music store and try out guitars that I couldn't afford to buy. I took strolls in parks and relaxed on park benches where I would lose myself in thought. I hiked to beautiful places by rivers, lakes, seashore, or into the hills and mountains of the Pacific Northwest. And one of these times, when I was in a quiet, beautiful, peaceful place, I had my first talk with the "Old One."

The Christian Bible says that God spoke to everyday people. Some were humble fishermen. How did God do this? Did God appear in a vision before them? Some religions believe that God sent angels as messengers to their prophets, and it was the angels who brought God's messages. Did God put them in a trance and guide their hand as they wrote? Did God simply put thoughts into their minds, and then those thoughts were written and eventually became part of the holy books? Did God put thoughts into their minds as dreams? I was about to find out for myself.

It was summer 2007, and my flight took me to Medford, Oregon on a gorgeous summer day. The approach to the Medford airport from the north passes over a large, square, flat-topped butte. There is a trail to the top, and that day I decided to take that hike. The view to the south was beautiful! The Rogue River twisted its way near the foot of the butte, and the cities of Central Point, Medford and Ashland stretched off toward the pass through the Siskiyou Mountains of northern California. I sat there near the edge of a cliff reveling in the beauty of that spectacular vista! Halfway reclining on a soft patch of grass that was pleasantly comfortable, I looked up at the deep blue sky, in which a few white, puffy clouds were slowly drifting by. I leaned back and found that the slope of the ground was just right to support my back and head as if I were sitting in a recliner at home in my living room. I closed my eyes and let my thoughts go wherever they happened to go. I didn't try to focus my thoughts on any one thing. Then I began to think back to when I first began to wonder whether there might really be a God that brought all this beauty I saw around me into existence.

I recalled the time when I was four years old and blurted out the phrase, "My God, look at this!" I had found a ball of string and was excited because now my father could show me how to fly the kite I had just been given. Why the word God popped out of my mouth I can't explain. My parents and sisters' reaction made me feel so ashamed for saying it that I thought God must be something bad, something to fear!

Many years had passed since that puzzling event. I had gone through several iterations of what my concept of God was. I had some religious instruction and exposure to Christianity when I was a child and teenager, but I always knew that I had doubts—and feelings of guilt and fear of the jealous, angry God. But couldn't it be that God is neither angry nor jealous but wise, calm, patient and approachable; if such a Being even exists.

So that day on the butte, I thought, "Why not try talking to God?" And that day I began my conversations with Old One through my thoughts. Yeah, I know many people who read this will say that I don't actually talk to God, but simply create my own thoughts of Old One conversing with me. While I don't care at all what anyone says, I too wonder if I actually converse with Old One in my thoughts, or if it is my imagination creating the dialogue. I have decided that I really don't know, but that no one else knows either. To those who choose to tell me that I am creating these thoughts myself, I say, "Prove it to me," and beyond that I don't care at all if you scoff at me, laugh at me, or tell me that I'm crazy. I simply choose to believe that perhaps Old One is answering my questions, just as other people who think there is no Creator choose to maintain that belief.

That gorgeous day on the butte when I begin to converse with the Old One, I formed the thought in my mind: "Will you speak to me, Old One?" I immediately received an answer in the form of what I call a voice-thought: "Why sure! I certainly will. All you need to do is think of what you want to say to me. And—you only need to think that it may happen—not believe it without any doubt—just be willing to think that maybe it is possible. But you guessed one very important thing about what I am like. I don't ever become angry!"

The voice was very soft, soothing, gentle, yet resonant. Somehow, it was entirely gender neutral. Hearing it, thinking it, whichever it was, caused me to feel utterly unafraid and at perfect peace. I was awestruck! A man like me—a nobody—talking with the Creator of all. I didn't know what to say or ask next. I was awed and speechless.

Then Old One said to me, "I'll help you to get started talking with me. After you get used to it, you will find it much easier to carry on a conversation. If you ask questions, I won't always answer your questions directly. Sometimes I won't answer your questions at all. Sometimes, I will answer by showing you an event or events that occurred sometime in the past or asking you a question to which you may already know the answer but don't realize it, or to which know the answer but don't like it. I'll start things off by reworking what many people on your

Earth call the "Ten Commandments," which I supposedly presented to someone (maybe I did, maybe I didn't) long ago in the past. Well, those commandments have been around for many years, and much has changed in the world in which you live, so they need to be elaborated upon.

"Some of these changes are actually corrections because the people who wrote them long ago didn't always follow my words exactly. They often added their own words. Sometimes those writers meant well. Sometimes there were translations done by people who were ordered to write what those in power thought would cause more fear of terrible punishments if the commandment was disobeyed. Often, they wrote what the person who had power over them ordered them to write, and thus the religious leaders, priests, shamans—whatever they were called—increased power and influence over their followers."

Chapter 13
Old One Reworks the Ten Commandments

"All right," Old One said, "I'll get started. The First Commandment: 'You shall have no other gods before me.' I didn't really say that. Somebody threw that in because they thought that all rulers should demand that their subjects bow before them and would punish horribly anyone who didn't bow down before them, refused to practice the official religion, or either disrespected or insulted them. You figured me out: I don't get angry. That's what you humans do. I don't need any of you humans to tell me how all-powerful, mighty and merciful I am—I know what I am.

"What is good about that 'no other gods before me' commandment? Think of it as meaning this: don't pursue wealth or power like it is a God. Some of you do that just so you can say to yourself or the other people around you, 'Look at me! I'm richer than you,' or 'I am the boss and have the power to tell you what to do.' People may line up and pretend to admire and love you to gain favors or just to see you wave and smile as you ride by in a chauffeured limo. All that really amounts to nothing but what you commonly call 'an ego trip,' isn't it?

"Many of you don't, in your own deepest thoughts, believe in yourselves. You gain a sense of self-worth by being in a position of power over other people. Then you can dispense favors and people will cater to you to gain favors. Many people gain their sense of self-worth by attaining a position that they consider is important; they feel that it's 'important to be important.' There are those who become 'important' without a thought or a care of being recognized by others as being 'important'; people such as these are concerned only with doing something of value that benefits humanity. People who want to become 'important' only to inflate their sense of self-worth are not worthy of my respect. Some people devote themselves to education and hard work and may become wealthy by filling a niche or a need or starting a new business that employs many people. That's okay by me! However, flaunting one's wealth is not good, doing so does not benefit humanity; it causes resentment in those who have achieved or earned less. People that flaunt their wealth (or pretended wealth) do it only because they don't have a sense of self-worth.

"Such people should remember that the ones who are fawning over them don't really care about them at all; the attention with which they are being showered is only with the expectation of receiving some benefit. There is an expression for this in Washington DC, the capitol of the United States: 'If you want a friend in Washington, get a dog.'

"I know what each person is thinking when they 'pray' to me, tell me how almighty, powerful and merciful I am, and how much they love me. Usually, they are saying those words because they hope I will be pleased and therefore grant whatever they are asking me to do or keep me from being angry with them. I'll say it again: I don't get offended or angry.

"That's enough for our first conversation," said Old One. "I know that you have things to get done and you need to get busy doing them. Any time you want to talk with me just send me a thought. I'll know if it's a good time to answer, if it is, I'll answer, if not, try again. I'll finish updating those Ten Commandments. We'll talk about many things. Just send me thoughts. I'll answer when you call, and I know that circumstances are right."

*****

Several months passed before I thought about asking Old One to talk again with me. I was on a night flight from Boise, Idaho, to Seattle, Washington, in January. It was cold and sparkling clear. I had climbed to my planned cruise altitude of ten thousand feet, levelled off and completed the cruise checklist. Once past Ontario, Oregon, off on the left wing, the terrain was sparsely populated. The airway parallels

Interstate 84 closely enough that I could see the headlights of cars and trucks creeping along. The only towns of any size between Ontario and Pendleton, Oregon, were Baker City and La Grande, which stood out as distant clusters of lights. There was no moon so the sky was black except for the pinpricks of light made by more stars than I could ever count. The only illumination in the cockpit was on the instrument panel.

Often, when I was fortunate enough to find myself in conditions like these, I would gradually dim the instrument lights to the lowest level that I could safely monitor them and then also pick out a star or constellation to home in on to maintain heading. With the cockpit lights dimmed, my night vision became more acute and the view of the vast ocean of stars even more awesome. I marveled at the scene, and the steady low rumble of the engines lulled me until it seemed that I was in another space—another dimension—a glimpse into eternity. I thought of the home of all humanity, Earth, a sphere rotating in the infinity of space. And then, the thought came to me: "Old One, did I imagine our first conversation or was it real?"

Immediately there was a response: "Yep, it was real. I'll pick up now where I left off, reworking the Ten Commandments. Okay now, Commandment Two has to do with people worshipping images. I don't really care about that. Way back thousands of years ago, it probably helped people get on the same track and not fight about which image was the right one or the one that would not offend me. You people need to stop worrying about offending me. I don't get offended. I don't become angry!

"Commandment Three is about taking my name in vain. Do you people even actually know what my name is, or that I even have a name? If I were to get angry—and remember I don't—there are many things people do that would arouse my ire more than someone saying 'God dammit' when something happens that displeases them. Maybe they were driving a nail and hit their thumb and it hurt a whole bunch. I say it again: I don't get offended or angry.

"Commandment Number Four is to remember the Sabbath day and keep it holy. Oh yeah, and I created the whole shebang, the entire universe of which you humans are aware, in six days and then relaxed for a day. Well, it took me a lot longer than your seven days to create what you call the universe, but the creation story was told in terms that could be understood in its own time. If you choose to believe that I created the whole works in six of your days and relaxed on the seventh of your days or a zillion of your years, I could care less! The holiness part of Sabbath Day, though, should be every day of your lives. You keep your days holy by treating your fellow humans with kindness and respect."

My headset crackled with the voice of the Salt Lake Center controller handing me off to Seattle Center.

"That's all for now," said Old One. "Next time we talk, I'll rework Commandment Five, there's a lot to say about this one!"

*****

I woke up in the crash pad that the company provides for pilots to rest between flights. This crash pad was one of the better ones, and it would be great bachelor quarters. It was small, about five hundred square feet—essentially one big room—with a three-quarters-high wall separating a sleeping area from the living-dining-kitchen area. Off the sleeping area was a tiny bathroom. It was about two miles from the I-5 freeway on a country road to the south of the small village of Gold Hill, Oregon. It might have been a mother-in-law dwelling at one time. It's very quiet and peaceful, at the foot of a steep hillside covered with a forest of Pacific madrone trees. We had a madrona in the yard where we lived for thirty-five years. In the Seattle area they are called madrona. They make for shade, but other than that, they're a nuisance because they're always doing something. They never shed their leaves all at once but gradually, all year long, with just enough leaves that raking never ceased. And if the continual sloughing of leaves wasn't enough, the bark peeled and fell off. The madronas grew blossoms that fell off and then made berries that fell off. There was no end to their activities and the need for cleanup. As a final insult, hardly anything would grow under them.

I had awakened, strolled out onto the narrow deck, glanced at the time on my cell phone, and seen that I had about two hours until I had to be at the airport for the evening flight back to Seattle. Still a bit groggy from sleep, I settled into a deck chair sitting under the madrone trees. My thoughts focused on checking in with Old One.

Immediately, Old One spoke: "Time to update Commandment Five, which says to honor your father and your mother. I have some important comments regarding this one. Certainly no one would have been born if two humans hadn't had sex and caused a baby to be created by a male and a female. Every person should be grateful that this miracle of conception through birth happened. From there on, however, this business of honoring your father and mother depends entirely upon whether the parents are deserving of being honored. Many babies are born without their parents even wanting them or considering before creating them if they have the means to care for them. Babies are born and then neglected; do those parents deserve to be honored? NO! Some people abuse their children; should those parents be honored? Absolutely not! Couples sometimes have children, but then try to make their children objects of great success so they can boast of their children's accomplishments. Should those parents be honored? Parents sometimes push their child or children into a profession so they can crow about their child the doctor, lawyer or some other highly prestigious position. Children then find themselves forced into having to spend their lives working at an occupation which they detest. Do their parents deserve to be honored? Parents who somehow bring out the best of their children's capabilities and help them succeed in a fulfilling occupation as they mature into adults are the parents who truly deserve being honored."

This brought to mind several incidents which I had fallen into during my life. I was on a Friday evening airline flight from Chicago to Seattle, a plane load of business people—probably many just like me—going home after a week away from home. I was in a window seat. The middle seat was empty, the aisle seat occupied by a well-dressed, middle-aged man. I noticed that he appeared to be arranging a class schedule, which I thought might be his own. When I asked him if he was pursuing further education, he said, "Oh no, my daughter is a straight-A student. She's way too busy studying to do this, so I'm helping her out by making up her class schedule."

His manner of speaking had a tone of arrogant superiority about it that made me wonder if his daughter was allowed to decide for herself what goal she wanted to pursue. Did she dream of becoming an actress, entertainer, or writer? Or was Daddy forcing her into a career that would give him much to boast about? Remembering this event, many years later, I only hope that her life has turned out well; that she wasn't forced to abandon a dream. I hope that her life didn't fall into disastrous shambles of rebellion, running from parental pressure and perhaps becoming a victim of drugs, alcohol or suicide, as sometimes happens when children are not allowed to follow their passion.

The second incident occurred many years later. I had met with another pilot for breakfast. He was a middle-aged man who had been laid off from a well-paid job with a semi-conductor manufacturer when the economy turned down. During the conversation, I asked if he had children; to which he replied that he had a daughter in college. I asked what she was studying and his response upset me. He told me that she wanted to study photography, but he had insisted that she get a degree in business so she would have greater opportunity of a good job. I responded by telling him how I resented my parents doing all they could to discourage my dreaming of becoming an airline pilot. I asked if he would want his daughter to feel that way about him later in life. It made an impression on him. Sometime later we met, and I asked if he had told his daughter to go for her dream. He said that he had. I don't know the end of this story; our paths haven't crossed again. I hope all has gone well for both of them.

And one more story. A wonderful lady who loves animals, particularly dogs and, after earning a bachelor's degree, master's degree, and a doctorate from prestigious universities, now follows her dream and runs a dog-sitting business. Finally, after years spent on education and employment in her field, she is living her dream. She was pushed into the higher education route by parental pressure and made Daddy very proud; and she does feel satisfaction from what she achieved. At last she is living her dream running a dog care business. I'm so happy for her.

Old One spoke again, "All this applies to adoptive parents as well, or to people who are simply acting as parents. What matters in your lives? Being a decent person, being honest, caring for other people's feelings, and following an occupation in life that is personally rewarding and contributes to the betterment of humanity. If parents are successful in raising children to this end, they are truly worthy of being honored. A word of caution here to young people: I know if parents are worthy of being honored, so in your youthful rebelliousness of growing up, don't think you can fool me as to whether or not your parents deserve your honor. Remember that parents are human beings who can make mistakes, I know when they are trying to do the best they can in raising their children."

"Commandments six, seven, eight and nine shouldn't need any rework; they are plain old common sense that I have given you humans; however, too often people of one belief or another use their beliefs to break or disobey these commandments, so I'll talk about them.

"Commandment Six: You shall not kill. Killing—murdering other people—is often justified by those who mistakenly believe they are pleasing me by eliminating those of different beliefs. I (God, Allah, Brahma, Jehovah, Odin, Old One, whatever name you choose to call me) am never pleased when murder is committed to silence those of a different religious belief. Killing other human beings sometimes cannot be avoided in certain cases where one is defending oneself or another, but I know when this is so. There is no fooling me!

"Commandment Seven: You shall not commit adultery. Those who break this commandment and are discovered cause great emotional pain to others. So, it is a form of theft because it is stealing another person's happiness.

"Commandment Eight further forbids stealing." You shall not steal." There are many ways to steal. The most obvious, of course, is taking some material thing that the thief well knows belongs to another person. Another way occurs when those who are capable of providing for themselves instead choose to beg and receive help from others. That person is stealing wealth from those who truly cannot help themselves: Shame on them! There are other ways to steal, such as when those of one belief system destroy property belonging to another, which they deem to be 'wrong.'

"Destroying property that must be rebuilt is actually stealing from all those who have to contribute their personal wealth to rebuild. Such destruction is often carried out in my name, which does not please me. Another way of stealing is through threats and acts of violence against those of different beliefs, which you call 'terrorist threats.' Much wealth must be spent to guard against these threats, and that wealth so spent is stolen from other human needs.

"Commandment Nine: You shall not bear false witness against another person. This applies not only to falsely accusing another person of a crime; it also applies to falsehoods told about someone else for one's personal gain or to elevate one's self-esteem. This is theft of a sort, stealing someone else's reputation, or lying to deprive another person of some benefit."

"And finally, Commandment Ten: 'You shall not covet.' It's okay to admire another person's possessions (including spouses), but it's not okay to envy another person's possessions that were acquired and achieved through honest efforts. It is okay to work to better one's situation in life, or to feel proud of oneself for accomplishing a task or attaining a goal, but a person should not do things simply to be able to boast that he or she has done better than everyone else.

"These commandments were never necessary. They can be summed up into one simple statement: 'Do unto others as you would have them do unto you.' That simple statement has been around for a long, long time. The commandment about having to worship me isn't needed; I know what I am, and as I said, every day should be holy. Too many people who go to worship me, tell me how almighty, all powerful, compassionate and merciful I am on the so-called Sabbath day, but then treat their fellow humans unkindly the rest of the week."

"That's enough for now," Old One said. "Next time we talk, I'll take you on a trip through time and space that I know you'll find fascinating."

These encounters with Old One left me in awe and with so much to think about that I had to take time between visits to assimilate what I had been told. I was still unsure if these conversations were real; yet, whenever I called up Old One, a response usually came.

Chapter 14
Journey through Time and Space

In a Cessna 172, four-place single, it was a forty-five-minute trip from Boeing Field in south Seattle to Port Angeles on a clear day. That flight was usually a pleasant break from flying over the Cascade Mountains to Spokane or Pasco in eastern Washington, when during the winter months I often had to deal with turbulence and icing. However, today wasn't a clear day: not even close. Pouring rain was punctuated by wind gusts. It was the same thing at Port Angeles, but a bit worse. It would be an instrument approach for certain, which usually added thirty minutes to the trip. This morning was not as usual. There were three airplanes ahead of me for landing, and the controller ordered me to hold at eight thousand feet with two other planes holding below, waiting to be cleared for the approach. Fortunately, while climbing to eight thousand feet, the rain became dry snow, so there wasn't a threat of icing. Eventually, I was cleared for the approach and was able to land. The normally forty-five-minute flight had taken over an hour and a half. After unloading the freight to the couriers, I headed to McDonald's for a breakfast of a sausage biscuit with egg, my monthly allowance of junk food. I was tired, but on that day sleeping at the crash pad wasn't appealing. I'd find a place to park and sleep in the car. That day I drove toward the Coast Guard Station at the end of the long spit called Ediz Hook. I parked the car heading north facing the Strait of Juan de Fuca. It was still raining, and the wind was blowing quite hard, causing the seas to crash against the breakwater rocks and throw spray high into the air. I watched until I drifted off to sleep. When I woke about an hour and a half later, the storm had moved to the east, and the seas had calmed somewhat. As the cobwebs of sleep cleared away, my thoughts came into focus, and I thought of calling up Old One. Immediately, Old One responded with, "Got some questions for me?"

"Wow! Old One, there are so many questions that come to mind that I don't know what to ask first. I'll ask this first because your answer will determine which questions I won't bother asking. I think I already know what your answer will be. Will you answer questions regarding the future? I expect your answer will be 'no.'"

Old One chuckled and said, "You're right, I won't answer questions about your future or the future of the world you live in. You want me to tell you when you will leave your earthly body, or 'die' as you humans call it? You don't really want to know the answer to that question, do you? Would you like to know another reason I won't answer questions about the future? Because you wouldn't be able to keep from monkeying around to try and change the future I told you about. Tell you what, I know what interests you, so I'll take you on a journey through time and space. Are you ready? Here we go."

The sensations I experienced were unlike anything I had ever experienced before and so hard to describe. Light, dark, flashes of brilliant colors, temperature changes yet never uncomfortably so, noise, a cacophony of noise yet somehow musical and beautifully pleasant, soothing, comforting. Pleasant scents and tastes. All my senses were stimulated but never harshly. Time seemed to stand still and yet rush by, and all through this journey I knew Old One was there taking me someplace, somewhere, to help me understand and for me to learn. And then we were there, somewhere, the first of many stops in this journey conducted by Old One.

Old One said, "Watch, you are going to see how I created the universe."

Suddenly—at least it seemed sudden to me—I was immersed in indescribably brilliant light. I could sense this light without really seeing it; it was visible and yet it somehow wasn't. I felt as though wrapped in a soft, cuddling, warm blanket.

Old One spoke: "You are witnessing the beginning of what you call the universe. Just watch as I take you through its evolution. It doesn't matter to me if anyone believes it took me six of your days or that it took me billions of your years. Most of the books that various beliefs call 'holy' were written long ago in your past, long before any humans had figured out that your Earth is a sphere rotating in space. What I am going to show you was unimaginable to the humans of those times."

Then it was totally, utterly black and quiet like I had never before experienced, with no light, no sound, no temperature, yet not uncomfortable. There was nothing to hear, touch, taste or smell. Only absolute, total nothingness. Then I began to see brief sparkles and flashes of light as Old One spoke.

"This is the beginning of your universe. I created these tiny disturbances in empty space."

Space was no longer empty. The smallest of these disturbances began to connect with others to form more tiny entities, and there was a building up of larger and larger things, which combined into more complex things until all that we are made of and have learned about and that we have not yet discovered came into existence. Old One made it possible for me to observe the creation of the most fundamental entities of all that we humans have discovered, and the combining of those into the building blocks of what we perceive to be matter and light.

"The ones you call scientists," Old One said, "have learned and discovered only a tiny part of what I have created and how it happened. They will find out much more. They will never discover and understand it all. Some of what they have learned is correct, some is not; but I caused to come into existence all of which you are aware and all of which has yet to be discovered. As I said, you have just begun to learn. You humans are but one among an infinity of life in the Infinite Universe. I'll tell you what life is because it may exist in environments that you humans would consider impossible, as you are beginning to discover. Life exists in places on your earth where not long ago it was thought impossible for life to exist. You've have heard of the creatures living near the fumaroles deep under the sea."

"So, what is life?" I asked Old One.

"What is life? Old One responded, "It is actually quite simple; it is an arrangement and combination of the 'stuff' where it exists, that reproduces itself. Intelligent life is aware of its own existence. I'll tell you of a place in which you humans think it impossible for life to exist; deep inside what you call stars. Is it impossible for what I have defined as life to exist there? Perhaps the life spans of whatever life exists within stars will have life spans that to you humans would seem unbelievably short because of the extremely high temperatures and therefore the rapid motion of the 'stuff' of life. Maybe life exists there; maybe it doesn't; I want to leave questions for you humans to try to find answers. You humans have so much yet to learn!"

"Now," Old One said, "I'm going to put the evolution of the universe and of you humans on Fast Forward. Some of you humans believe that I have existed forever but made everything in only six of your days. I ask those people, what do you think I was doing before I created your universe in six of your days? How did I pass that infinite amount of time before I created your universe that some of you believe equals a few thousand years in the past? Do you humans think that I created universes other than the one in which you reside? Some of your scientists think that the universe is infinite. Some think that other universes exist. Are they right? That's another question for you humans to ponder.

"So now, you can watch the creation of your universe, including the first humans. Was the universe you perceive started as a 'Big Bang' as many of your great cosmologists believe, or has it always existed? Maybe your universe has been "expanding" for an infinite period of time and will do so for an infinity of the time you humans experience. Remember that I exist in all of your human times. Time for me does not exist. Will your universe expand forever and the atoms in it expand while maintaining the same size ratio between universe size and the atoms? These are some of the many questions for you humans to try to answer, and that is how I intend it to be. I know that you have wondered if the universe in which your planet Earth exists is like an atom in a

108

vastly larger universe, and the things you call atoms in your universe are miniscule complete universes. You wonder if everything keeps going up in size and also down in size. I won't tell you the answer. It's just another question for you humans to ponder: infinity up and down, bigger and smaller, ad infinitum, never ending."

"Old One, please help me understand," I pleaded.

And Old One gave me the capability to understand what I watched unfolding before me. It wasn't like seeing with my eyes. It was as if Old One was pouring knowledge into my mind. The flashes of light I sensed were the most fundamental bits of all that humans who study such things consider to be real. They combined to become composite entities that combined further into the simplest atoms. Then my awareness was viewing a vast sea of these atoms, filling all space with a total uniformity.

Old One said, "Now watch what happens when I stir things up a bit." The uniformity began to break up into swirls and eddies. These discontinuities became more and more distinct, and then one lit up and became what Old One told me was the birth of the very first star in our universe. Another star began to burn, then another, and another and then there were countless stars. Old One changed the time scale, and I watched the evolution of the universe proceed faster and faster as stars 'turned on' and began assembling themselves into galaxies of billions of stars and galaxies into forming into clusters.

"Just to keep you humans guessing," Old One said. "Maybe that's how it all began or maybe all the 'stuff' that comprises everything you humans live with has always existed, like I have always existed. Some of you humans think that it all began from nothing. Maybe this is so, but maybe not. Maybe everything that makes up the universe has existed forever and just keeps rearranging itself. I won't tell you the answers. Many people wouldn't believe me if I did."

"Hey, watch now," Old One said. "Here's the beginning of the tiny part of the universe in which you live."

I saw gases and dust swirling, forming eddies, which grew and began to glow with a light that was barely perceptible at first. It gradually changed to a deep red, though still quite faint. Then the red became brighter and segued into orange, then yellow, which shone brighter and brighter, then yellow-white, and I realized a star had been born. More and more eddies grew and brightened and became stars. The galaxy that we humans call home was forming. Time accelerated again, and Old One told me to focus on one particular star, which was surrounded by a disc of dust and gas. The disc rotated with the star-sun, but again eddies formed, and the matter comprising the disc clumped together into spheres of different sizes. Old One zoomed in on a tiny part of the scene I saw unfolding and directed me to watch one of the spheres.

"That is the beginning of your Earth," Old One said.

I was fascinated and choked with emotion as I saw our planet being born. It was nothing like the Earth we know today. It was a fiery orange-red ball. It grew and grew as it was bombarded with the debris of our solar system in its infancy. A sphere of about one-fourth of Earth's diameter was approaching the planet, and it struck with a glancing blow and careened off. Then, it had lost so much of its speed that it began to orbit Earth. Earth's moon had assumed its place circling Earth and had left a gouge on one side of the planet's orb that one day, far in the future, would be the Pacific Ocean. Old One speeded up my perception of Earth's formation. As it was cooling, the crust began to form. Then there was cloud cover. When the clouds began to break up, and I could begin to see Earth's surface, there was one large landmass and the blue seas. During the time of the cloud cover, it had rained for thousands of years and filled the oceans with life-giving water. Old One now changed my vision so I could see what was happening in the depths of the ocean.

"Old One, will you show me how you created life?"

"Watch carefully now," Old One said, "And you will witness the beginning of all life on your earth."

I watched, fascinated. I realized that what I was seeing was taking place over many millions of human years, but Old One was moving me through time, space and giving me the ability to see what was occurring at atomic and molecular levels, the tiniest beginnings of life. Atoms joined to form molecules, molecules joined and became larger molecules, and then one of the larger molecules began to elongate. It stretched out into an oval shape, then into a long, slender shape, and then it pinched in the middle and split into two identical copies of the original one. Each part then gathered other molecules and atoms from the liquid in which it was immersed, until each of the two halves had become like the original molecule that had divided into two parts.

Old One chuckled and said, "You just witnessed the beginning of life on your earth. I didn't actually cause that molecule to divide. I just thought the universe into existence and knew what would happen; so, it's okay to say that I caused it. You humans, or some of you humans who believe I exist, also believe that I know everything past, present and future. For me, then, there is no time. Everything happens at once."

John Archibald Wheeler was right!

Old One guided me through different degrees of magnification; sometimes down to miniscule size, sometimes at a field of view that encompassed the entire Earth, our Milky Way Galaxy, and more. Old One showed me things that I didn't understand, like many different modes of vibrating somethings. I asked what they were, and I could sense that Old One was amused.

"If I tell you the answers to the many questions you have, there will be less for you humans to figure out for yourselves, and I know that some of you enjoy the challenge of finding out for yourselves. Some want to solve such problems. Others don't, and either way is all right. Think of how it would be if all of you were interested in the same thing."

As I watched, I saw the tiny, single-celled things that copied themselves sometimes join with others. Then there were larger living things. I saw the beginning of creatures that crawled on the sea floor and swam through the water. From a vantage point out in space where Old One had taken me, I saw the Earth change form. Land masses drifted around and collided, and when this happened I saw mountain ranges being pushed up, and then Old One made time flow more rapidly, and I saw those same mountains eroded away by the wind and rain and washed into the sea. Land masses still moved and mountains were again forced up. Land masses collided to form continents, broke apart, and collided again.

I marveled as I watched this ever-changing Earth evolve from one form to another. Land masses were pushed up above sea level; other areas sank below sea level and filled with water. Rivers flowed to the sea and cut channels and deep canyons in the Earth. They carried sediment to the sea and formed river deltas. The sea and lakes were continually building up sedimentary layers in the earth. Huge volcanoes erupted, smothering the earth in smoke and ash; they blocked out the sunlight and caused dramatic climate change. Life forms that couldn't adapt or find shelter became extinct, their remains sometimes becoming entombed in sediment, leaving a record that they once lived and thrived. Meteors, striking the earth and throwing vast quantities of debris into the atmosphere, brought about severe changes in climate and extinctions of life. All these changes over millions of years left a record of the earth's history. Complex living creatures arose from simpler living creatures. Sometimes a change in a living creature would happen just by chance and thereby give an advantage to that creature in the competition for survival. It would then be more likely to survive and reproduce, giving it an edge over other creatures. I saw life forms change from tiny microscopic creatures to a fantastic collection of animals, birds, reptiles, fishes, including some gigantic ones. The earth and the seas also harbored a myriad assortment of plant life, again ranging in size from microscopic to huge sequoia-like trees. Once again, darkness flooded over the earth.

The climate changed dramatically and much of the life that I had watched arise and evolve—died! Sunlight began to warm the earth again. Life started again on its never-ending struggle to survive, to adapt to whatever its environment became. I was awestruck as I saw creatures evolve. After an event that caused the extinction of many creatures, I saw how new and different creatures arose and adapted to the different environment. Some species succeeded and thrived, crowding out those that were not as well suited. This sequence of events repeated itself several times, and each time many of the living things on earth became extinct. But as conditions changed, living things again arose from their surroundings, adapted to conditions, and evolved into creatures better suited to their environments.

Old One showed me a creature that I didn't recognize in the least. Then Old One said, "Watch as I speed up the changes to the descendants of this ancient creature as it evolves over eons of time."

It was like a slow-motion movie shown frame by frame. Old One was showing me the evolution of the creature. In slow motion I could watch tiny changes take place in the countless generations of this creature.

Old one said, "Now I'll speed this up so you will see what it is in your time." I looked and saw what it had become, heard Old One chuckle and ask me, "What do you see?"

What I saw caused me to burst into laughter. I recognized one of the strangest creatures on this earth—a duck-billed platypus. The duck-billed platypus is the most mixed-up creature on earth that has been discovered by humans because it is an egg-laying furry mammal that sweats milk for its young and has the bill of a duck, the tail of a beaver, webbed feet like an otter, and poisonous barbs on its hind legs.

Old One chuckled again and said, "When it was first discovered, learned people who studied such things believed it to be a hoax."

Leading me on this fantastic journey and exhibiting a sense of humor, Old One made me feel totally unintimidated by all I experienced. I lost all hesitancy regarding our relationship; I could converse about anything; I knew that whatever I said or asked would not offend or anger Old One.

Chapter 15
Distant Ancestors

I had awakened from a much needed, four-hour sleep in the crash pad at Idaho Falls. I was still drowsy and my thoughts wandered to Old One and the journey through time and space. What's next, Old One, I wondered.

Old One responded immediately. "The scenes of the past that I will show you now will help you understand the ascent of humans from brutes to caring people. You will also see how some humans committed cruel acts for their own benefit—to attain and maintain power."

Then I found myself in a cave, where a small group of humanlike beings gathered around a small fire near the entrance. I could feel the somewhat cool temperature and smell the smoke from their fire. There was a musty odor—a blend of moss, lichen and mold—and moisture glistened on the rough cave walls. Old One said, "These beings are very early humans, the ones your people who study such things have called 'Cro-Magnons.'"

They were communicating through gestures and sounds that I could not understand until Old One translated for me. I listened as Old One told me they were discussing fire, which they were just beginning to use. One of them told some others that he had discovered how to create fire. I gathered from the reaction of the others that instead of being impressed by his discovery, the group considered him to be foolish and troublesome. They pointed out that he often suggested or tried out new and different ways of doing things, and clearly that bothered them.

Old One told me that the others often laughed at the foolish one's ideas because his ideas often didn't work as he hoped they would. But he never stopped trying. And because he never gave up trying, he was able to solve problems more easily than the others, which made some of them jealous and resentful.

The foolish-troublesome raised his voice above the jeers and guffaws of the others. He told them that now they wouldn't have to wait for the magic powers to cause lightning to strike the earth or a dead tree, which would then create fire. He described how he had created a glowing ember by rubbing pieces of wood together very fast; then, by gently blowing upon it and applying fine bark shavings, he had made fire. This story he told made the others, complete with hand gestures, only made them laugh even louder.

But one older being, who appeared to be the biggest and most muscular, and who seemed to be the group's leader, sat quietly and listened. Then he raised his hand as a command for the laughter and jeering to stop. Everyone immediately fell silent, and then the leader spoke. The others bowed their heads slightly out of respect and fear of the leader. The leader spoke slowly and carefully. He said that while such a fire-starting method might work, it must not be used, must be forgotten and never again mentioned or discussed. Only fires started by the unknown, unseen, magic powers that sent lightning could be used.

The group leader said that if the troublesome one was actually able to make fire, it would anger the magic powers. The leader commanded the others to beat the foolish-troublesome one, but their victim broke free and ran from the cave into the fading twilight as they pelted him with stones. He fled from the group and never returned. He had learned that it was dangerous to speak of things that would be perceived as likely to anger the magical powers that made fire and caused wind, rain and the earth to sometimes shake and terrify them. And he had learned that some of his kind could make others obey them. They relished having this power over others, and they would do whatever they thought necessary to maintain their position of power.

Old One spoke again, "Now you will see how females were given no respect and were abused by the males. Some cultures of your present day treat females in the same way; they have not evolved past their cruel, primitive, and inconsiderate ways. They say their god decrees that males be in total control."

116

I saw that the females and children of the group were huddled in a lobe of the cave. I could sense their fear and frustration. (I could sense the emotions of the males as well, as though Old One was allowing me to see and know all there was to know about the clan.)

Old One said. "Females among that early human species had no status or power; they were treated as slaves. They were not considered to be of any value except to work and provide the males with sex on demand. They were not allowed to participate in activities considered to be only for males. The activity that was most forbidden was hunting. If they were allowed to take part in hunting, they would need to learn the use of weapons. The only weapon females were allowed to use were knives, so they could help with the butchering of slain animals. Males never spoke aloud of what most of them secretly feared—that if the females learned the skill of using weapons, they might rise up and use them against their male captors."

Dismayed by the brutality of the males, my sympathies were with the females. As I watched, I noticed that one of the female children, the eldest of those who had not yet reached puberty, watched the foolish-troublesome one being attacked by the rest of the males and was extremely upset. She had made up a name for the foolish-troublesome one; she called him a word that today means "kind." Kind seemed to be the only male who showed concern for those in pain. She had watched him ease the suffering of a male who had been terribly maimed by a wounded animal during a hunt. Even though the injured male soon died, Kind tried to ease the misery of his last minutes of life by giving him water; the other males did nothing. She had seen the other males cause more agony to dying animals hunted for food when they were near death by unnecessary cruel cutting and stabbing, but Kind would make them stop. Although he was among the biggest and strongest of the males, Kind was always protective of the smaller and weaker members of the clan, both males and females.

The young female had not been forced to have sex with one of the dominant males, and she dreaded the time when that might happen. As she knew, the captive females were brutally raped, often in full view of the others. She had seen Kind have sex with females, but he had never treated any of them in a brutal, uncaring manner as the other males did. If a female let him know that she didn't want sex, he would not insist, but would mate with a willing female. She regarded Kind as a very special male and hoped that he would choose her when she was ready to mate.

Now I found myself sympathizing with Kind and I saw things now from his point of view. The young female did not seem to know it, but Kind had noticed her. He kept close watch over her, just as she did over him. He had made up a name for her, which meant "bold." When she was ready for a mate, Kind hoped he would be the one, but he would never force himself on her. He knew he might have to fight the others to protect her from their brutality. Bold knew none of this but she longed to be with Kind and never with anyone else.

I noticed that Kind had watched her much more closely than she realized. He had seen her do forbidden things, which was why he had named her Bold. He had seen how she was kind to the crippled male who had been born with a deformed leg and often brought him food and water. The crippled one was allowed to live after reaching puberty only because he had developed a great skill for flint knapping, creating tools and weapons from rocks: hand axes, knives, spearheads. Because Bold was kind to him, the flint knapper made her knives and spearheads which she sneaked from the cave to a stealthy hiding place. Kind had hidden himself from view and watched her make spears of different weights and lengths. He watched her practice throwing them and thrilled to see her become more and more expert at hitting targets she set up. He saw her pantomime a fight with another person and could see she showed promise. What would she become when she reached her adult size? He had learned so much from his stealthy observations of her.

Meanwhile, I observed that Bold was watching out for Kind. One again I knew all that she was feeling and thinking. When the leader of the group commanded the males to beat Kind, Bold was terribly upset at first, but her anxiety turned to elation when she saw him break free and escape from the cave. She made a promise to herself that when everyone had gone to sleep for the night, she would track him down and find him. The thought of leaving the clan was terrifying. She had seen what the males had done to females who ran away. If the males tracked them down and brought them back, they would beat the runaway to near death. Kind had tried to stop this abuse, but he was the only male who intervened and was often overpowered by the other males and injured to some degree. Bold also knew she was risking her life by leaving the cave at night with hungry predators roaming outside, but she believed she was as skilled as any man in the use of spears and knives.

Bold forced herself to stay awake until she was certain that all the others were asleep. Her heart was pounding. Then, she quietly arose from her bed of animal furs, wrapping the largest one around her slender body, and slipped out of the cave. As she emerged from the cave, she was much encouraged that she might find him. The previous day a light dusting of snow had fallen, but the storm clouds had passed and a full moon shone brightly. Her heartbeat quickened because she could see the tracks that Kind had left and hoped they would lead her to him. First though, she detoured to the place where she had developed her spear-throwing skill to a point of perfection. She gathered the spears and knives that she had hidden and set forth.

She had not gone far before she was forcibly stopped by an arm encircling her throat and a hand covering her mouth. A male of the clan had been lying awake as she left the cave. He quietly followed her at a distance, waiting in the shadows as she gathered spears and knives from where she had hidden them. When her back was turned to him he caught her in his viselike grip. She had mentally and physically prepared herself for this very sort of attack. She bit down on one of the fingers of his hand covering her mouth; then both of her elbows jammed backwards into his rib cage, knocking the wind out of him. His arm fell from around her neck. She turned slightly and deftly kicked the back of his leg directly behind one of his knees, causing that knee to collapse and not support him. He began to fall. As he fell, she jerked his arm and made him fall on his back. Then as he lay on his back, wind knocked out of him, dumfounded that this young female had done this, she bent both of her knees fully; then, she intentionally fell, jamming both knees with all her weight into his breast bone. Several of his ribs broke, one ruptured his aorta.

"Did she kill him, Old One?"

"Yes, though she did not intend to. His blood pressure dropped to nothing, he lost consciousness immediately and bled to death internally."

I heard Old One sigh.

Bold picked herself up and collected her thoughts. She gathered her spears and decided to avoid passing near the cave entrance, in case any others had awakened and noticed that she or the male that she had killed were missing. She gave the cave entrance a wide berth and successfully found Kind's tracks. She knew she must follow them quickly because the temperature had risen above freezing, and the track would soon disappear. She walked and walked often looking back and to both sides to watch for hungry predators that she knew would catch her scent. The bright full moon helped. She had seen that she was being stalked by a predator. It was coming closer; as she looked back she would see a shadowy silhouette slinking from shadow to shadow. Fearful that it would soon attack her, she scanned her surroundings hoping to see a place where she could hide; that way if a predator was closing in on her she would have the advantage of surprise, giving her the chance to kill the predator.

She found the perfect place; two fairly large trees close enough together that she could crouch behind them, see between them, yet be almost entirely hidden. She could also hurl a spear between them when the predator came close enough. She crouched, watched and saw the predator; a young sabre-tooth tiger. It was near enough than to sense the warmth of her body and her scent and it was advancing toward her hiding place very slowly, a step, then a pause to raise its head and sniff the air. A perfect situation she thought. A few more steps toward her, and when it raised its head, she would hurl her spear, aiming just below its neck to try to hit its heart. She was tensed and ready. The sabre-tooth took one more step, raised its head and she threw the spear with all her strength. Her aim was on the mark. The spear penetrated deeply. The huge cat tried to roar, but the only sound from its throat was a mewling gurgle as blood poured from its mouth. It collapsed, thrashed on the ground for a few moments and then lay still, its sides heaving with its last breaths.

She left it there, knowing that the scent of its blood would keep other predators from following her trail, and began following Kind's tracks. She was so weary she had trouble staying on her feet at times, but her desire to find him kept her going. She would follow his tracks even if she had to crawl. Until she had not a breath of life left she would follow his trail.

As the full moon was sinking lower and the first glimmers of dawn were appearing in the east, she saw it: a shelter of fir boughs. She saw that Kind's tracks ended there and was sure he was sleeping beneath the boughs. She found the entrance to the shelter, and in the dim light of the breaking day she saw him.

When she touched his bearded face, he awoke with a start, opened his eyes and saw her gazing at him lovingly. He started to speak, but she put her fingers gently on his lips to silence him. She said softly, "Kind, I have named you, I have found you. Please don't send me away."

Kind parted the boughs that had covered him and kept him warm while he slept. He pulled her close to him, held her cold, shivering body pressed tight against him, and pulled the boughs back over them. He whispered to her, "Bold, the name I call you, I want you to stay with me for as long as I live. I will do all in my power to protect you and make you happy to be with me." As tears of happiness wet their cheeks, they clung to each other and slept.

Then I watched the rest of the couple's lifetime as if in fast motion. They stayed together. She grew into a statuesque, strong adult who developed many talents and skills. Kind marveled at her capabilities. They hunted together and once when they were on a hunt together, she saved his life. They were a short distance apart but within sight of each other. Kind was intent on stalking and killing a boar. Bold was watching with her spear ready to move in on the boar when she saw that Kind was being stalked by a large, wolf-like creature, which was crouching to pounce on him. Just as the wolf-creature began tensing its haunches to leap, Bold stood up in her hiding place and hurled her spear. Her spear pierced the wolf-creature's chest, and it collapsed in a thrashing of death throes.

Bold rushed to Kind, her voice choking out sobs of, "I could have lost you, I could have lost you!" They held each other until they had both calmed down. Kind was so proud of her. He helped her only when she asked for his thoughts on how to accomplish a task or develop a skill; he knew that she gained much satisfaction from solving a problem by herself. It never bothered him that she was better at some skills than he was. He delighted in seeing her successes.

They found an uninhabited cave, fought off aggressive cave males, but befriended the peaceable ones they met along the way. They had children and taught them all they knew, including how to be courageous and strong yet compassionate. And in their wanderings, they met others like themselves who had separated from groups that had been ruled by the strongest and cruelest. That is when those primitive beings first realized that they should not do to others that which they did not want done to themselves. Such a simple rule! Such an ancient beginning!

They grew old. Their bodies were wearing out and slowing down as happens to all living things. They had taught their children well, and so their children looked after them and helped them as they became older and feebler. Then, one night after they had drifted into sleep, first one and then the other passed out of the land of the living, as though the two of them had shared a single heart. Their children buried them, side by side, arms wrapped around each other, in a deep grave covered with large rocks to protect the bodies of the parents who had raised them well, taught them much.

Old One said to me, "Remember Commandment Five which I reworked? These were parents who truly deserved to be honored. This was the beginning of compassion, love and monogamy. Humanity still had far to go but this was a beginning. In that primitive society most males treated females as slaves, as property; it is done still in some societies of your time. Those in power say that it is commanded by God, however, they know but will never admit that it's their own way of keeping absolute control over women. They don't fool me. Old One knows."

Part III

Questions-Answers

Chapter 16
Tyranny-Beginnings

Old One and I began to travel through time again. I experienced the same potpourri of sensations, and then I witnessed another gathering of primitive people. They had just returned from a successful hunting party and were butchering a large animal and roasting large cuts of meat over an open fire. I could smell smoke and cooking meat; I could feel the fire's heat. I could hear voices, and it sounded like they were complaining about something. Old One translated for me so I could understand their conversations. Those doing the butchering were frustrated. The crude knives they were using to butcher were made of flint; they were not very sharp and often would break. Two of the men were arguing, and I gathered that one of the two was an elder, who was very skilled at flint knapping and made knives, axes, and spear points from stone. Having this skill gave him high status among the members of his clan. The other man had his own ideas, rather like the genius of a much earlier time who figured out how to make fire.

Old One showed me that the man arguing with the flint knapper was always busy, always trying different ways of making things, of finding a faster, better, easier way to accomplish whatever task needed to be done. He had noticed once, while tending a fire used for drying meat, that the stones placed around the fire pit, unusual greenish colored stones, seemed to vanish as the fire burned very close to them. This roused his curiosity, and he began working with the green tinted rocks and fire. After many trials his efforts paid off; he discovered a new material from which to fashion tools and weapons. He discovered it when he built a large fire on top of a pile of the unusual, greenish colored rocks. After the fire had burned to ashes and cooled, he was puzzled because the fire settled and the strange green rocks seemed to have vanished. He dug through the ashes and found an unfamiliar material that he could bend could slightly without breaking, unlike stone knives. The material was quite hard. He found that by pounding on it with a stone, he could shape it and make a sharp edge that was much better at cutting wood and butchering slain animals than any knife made of stone.

The flint knapper was very upset to learn of this discovery because it threatened his standing and prestige. He sneered at the foolish-troublesome one, who was becoming a big problem, others in the group seemed very interested. The flint knapper belittled him for suggesting that some material other than stone could be used to make knives, axes, arrow-heads and spear-points. Although some of the others joined in laughing and jeering at the foolish-troublesome one, there were many who were interested in hearing more about this new knife material.

Old One asked me, "You know what he discovered don't you?"

I responded, "I suspect it was copper. Is that right."

Old One said, "Yes it was copper. That was the beginning of you humans using metals."

Old One made it possible for me not only to understand the words being spoken but also to know the thoughts of the humans involved in this scene.

The flint knapper was in a state of panic. He could plainly see that the mysterious material that the know-it-all had discovered was far superior to the stone knives and axes that he flaked from flint-stone. His power and prestige were threatened. He must come up with a plan to preserve his position. He must somehow arrange for the Problem to be killed; and he knew of one who would help him make this happen—the shaman. The shaman was his brother who, along with a small group of the biggest and strongest, shared absolute power within the tribe.

The shaman had learned to behave in mysterious ways that caused the others to fear him and hold him in awe. He had learned clever tricks that the others believed were magical powers, which made them think his commands must be obeyed; this sort of behavior gave him power.

The flint knapper told his brother, the shaman, that the foolish-troublesome one had become a big Problem. He explained that he needed the shaman's help to get rid of the Problem.

"Let me think about it," the shaman replied. "I agree that the Foolish-Troublesome one has become a big problem. He has bewitched some our followers with his dangerous magic. It will take both of us and our most loyal assistants to rid ourselves of this Problem!"

The shaman thought long and hard about what to do. Some of the rituals that the shaman had contrived involved costumes intended to be frightening in appearance. He had created noisemakers of various types, rattles, drums, whistles, and horns. He had learned how to pulverize different materials, colored rocks, leaves, animal bones; into powder, which he would throw into fire to make smoke of different colors. He claimed it was magic and would either please or anger the many gods that were believed to control all that happened: illnesses, death, rain, wind, earthquakes, crop success or failure, and anything else that might happen.

He became an accomplished actor, and he had developed a wide variety of voices: low-pitched guttural, high-pitched screams, blood-curdling shrieks, and those in-between. One of the acts he put on was to behave as if he was being possessed by spirits that were taking control of his body, causing him to collapse, writhe on the ground, scream as if in agony, and speak in strange unintelligible tongues that no one else understood. He would utter sounds in one of his many voices that he would say was a language that he spoke when conversing with the gods or spirits. He had also gathered a small, group of young, easily influenced males to be his assistants and help him perform his rituals. They were given special benefits to insure their loyalty to him and his schemes. His plan to get rid of the Problem (the foolish-troublesome one) would use all of those skills, tricks, and helpers.

The shaman and flint knapper's plan began to take shape. The one who had made knives from this strange unknown material would be put on what would now be called a trial. All members of their clan must attend. The shaman and the flint knapper determined that the Problem's crime was angering the gods by creating knives from this strange new material. The shaman would claim to be speaking with the most powerful God and would utter sounds that only he and this supreme God understood. It must be very fearsome and impressive, so it would take place after dark. The fire and its flickering flames would be the centerpiece, with a large circle around it. Evenly spaced on this circle would be six smaller fires, each tended by one of his young assistants. Much smoke would be created by feeding green fir boughs onto the fires. The shaman would appear out of a cloud of smoke in his most frightening costume: the one with the head and hide of a leopard. The leopard's mouth had been fixed partly open with the fang-like canine teeth bared as if snarling, ready for attack. The leopard's eyes had been replaced with shiny stones which glittered in the firelight because the stones contained flakes of mica. The head fit snugly over the head of the shaman and he could see through the leopard's open mouth. As the shaman danced, quivered and gyrated he would move his head in all directions in jerky, spasmodic motions the firelight would reflect from the mica flakes in the eye stones giving an eerie appearance of a living, yet ghostly, being staring whichever way the head was turned and have a frightening effect upon those who would be watching the spectacle unfold—exactly the effect he wanted.

There were many in the clan who feared the flint knapper and his brother, the shaman. Most were fooled by the shaman's clever performances; they were convinced that the shaman conversed with the gods. They feared that the shaman would cause the gods to bring harm to them if they didn't obey any command issued by him. So, when the shaman ordered that the Problem be captured, placed in a cage and guarded until the time for his 'trial,' which would take place the same day after dark, the commands were carried out. The Problem was put into a cage, out-of-sight, a short distance away.

Daylight faded. Twilight slowly gave way to total darkness: there was no moon. The sky was clear and filled with stars. The only light came from flames of the flickering fires. The shaman's apprentices began drumming and shaking rattles. The unseen shaman's voice could be heard speaking in strange, unknown tongues, using many fearsome vocal tones, indicating that he was conversing with the gods. The fires were being fed green fir boughs to create smoke. The powders he made by pulverizing various stones were tossed into the fires, creating flashes of brilliant colors.

The drumming tempo increased to a frantic rate and then abruptly stopped. At that moment, the shaman sprang forth from a smoke cloud, clad in the frightening leopard skin garment, adorned with seashells strung on cords that rattled as he performed a ritual dance around the central fire. The drumming began again, slowly at first, then slowly increasing in tempo until he collapsed onto the ground, squirming and writhing as if in agony, quivering and shaking as if possessed until finally he lay still. The drumming stops. There is total silence.

After a short pause, the shaman stirs. He moans. He struggles to his feet. He screams, "The Gods have spoken to me! They are angry because one of us dared to disrespect the elder who has spent his life providing us with tools made from flint: the one who has claimed that a material other than flint is better. He must die for this disrespect! Bring him to me, drive stakes into the ground, and tie his wrists and ankles to the stakes. Everyone then must pass by and throw stones at him or cut or stab him with a flint knife. It must be done. If he lives the gods will send sickness upon us. We will all die."

But when they went to the cage, which was outside the circle of those who had watched mesmerized by the shaman's performance, it was empty. The Problem had escaped! He had hidden several of the knives of the new material beneath the animal skin clothing that he wore and easily cut the lashings which held the wooden bars together. The guards had become enthralled by the shaman's ritual and had gradually moved away from the cage to better watch. He escaped and left the clan, never to return. He roamed and met others like himself; those who were eager to search for better ways to accomplish tasks, explore the unknown, and question the existence and nature of gods.

"I have much more to show you," Old One said, and we began to travel through time again.

"Where are we going?" I asked.

"You will soon see."

Another scene began to appear to me. By now after two visits into the past, I expected Old One would translate for me or perhaps enable me to understand conversations in whatever language was being spoken. There were people gathered around watching. They were seated and watching someone who stood speaking to them. I could tell that the standing one was respected and feared by those who were sitting because of the way they would not meet his gaze whenever he would stare at one of them. He spoke of how he conversed with the magical powers that had become known as gods. He said that the gods had appointed him as their representative; everyone else must listen to him and obey his commands. He was to teach the others how they must behave, which included obeying him as their all-knowing leader. He said the gods had commanded him to order brutal punishments for those who refused to obey or even questioned his authority. He was known as the high priest.

But there was one who often questioned the representative's pronouncements, and he must be somehow gotten rid of. The representative decided to tell the group that the gods had commanded that the blasphemous one be killed. He couldn't have his power over the group lessen. If it did those in the group might no longer provide him with food, females, and other desires and necessities. They would no longer bow to him and tell him he was great and wise and powerful. He didn't actually believe that he was great and wise and powerful, which is why his ego needed others to tell him so. The blasphemous one must be gotten rid of immediately! The representative would tell the others in the group that the gods had commanded that the blasphemous one be stoned to death. So, it continued: the inhumanity of people to one another. It began with stoning people to death, but it would become much worse, Old One said.

The scene faded away. Old One said, "Remember what you have witnessed and learn from it. Although it is good to question beliefs and assumptions and to invent new ways to do things, it usually puts the person in peril, because they represent a problem to those in power."

We travelled through space-time again. Where in time and space would we go? What Old One would show me next?

Old One said, "What I am going to show you now is how those in power weren't interested in truth; they were interested in supporting whatever story they had been telling. If historical writings were found and translated but contradicted the established teachings, then the contents of those documents were discounted and suppressed, the documents destroyed, and those who had learned of those contents were imprisoned and often brutally killed. Pay attention now. You will see one such event."

A scene began appearing. It was a large room, lit only by candles and oil lamps. There were several long tables at which were seated a number of robed and hooded individuals. They were all hunched over writing with quill pens. They were scribes. Each scribe occupied a position which was equipped with an oil lamp or candles and an ink pot. I could feel the cool, damp air in the room brush my skin and catch the aromatic odor of the candles and oil lamps. An aura of fear bordering on terror pervaded the room. I could detect the somewhat salty scent of perspiration dampening the robes of the bent-over figures. The only sound was that of the rapid breathing stoked by fear and the scratching of the quill pens.

One seat was empty. It had been occupied by another foolish-troublesome one, and at this period of human existence any unorthodox behavior or ideas were quickly squelched. This scribe had been granted more tolerance because of his remarkable talent for translating the arcane scripts of ancient documents; however, lately his translations were not what those in power wanted to hear. The translations contradicted the teachings that those in power proclaimed were correct and must never be questioned. The foolish and troublesome one must be silenced—immediately!

Two very large, very brawny men, naked above the waist except for black leather hoods with eye holes, had taken the foolish-troublesome one away. The two were accompanied by a robed old man who ordered the victim to his feet. When the troublesome scribe-translator rose, the brawny hooded ones moved to either side of him. As they roughly grasped each of his arms, lifted him off his feet and started for the doorway through which they had entered, he began shouting, "You said for me to do an accurate translation. I thought you wanted to hear the truth—the truth—the truth!"

As he was dragged further and further away, down toward the dungeon-torture chamber, the other hunched scribe figures pretended not to hear, but they shuddered because they knew what fate was going to befall the one who had dared to tell those in power things that contradicted their pronouncements of truth. Doors were purposefully left open so they could hear his screams of agony. The robed old man who had come with the brawny ones remained after the victim was dragged away. He slowly paced behind the hunched-over figures who were scratching away frantically with their quill pens. The screams faded away to barely audible whimpers. Then, the brawny ones appeared, dragging the limp, apparently unconscious body of the foolish-troublesome one. The brawny ones moved toward a door that led outdoors into a public square, half dragging the limp form out into the square.

The old robed man had remained in the room with the hunched figures, and after the brawny ones were through the door, he spoke one word to them: "Outside." The scratching of the quill pens ceased immediately, and the scribes rose to their feet almost as one carefully synchronized motion. The older robed one stood by the door as they filed past going out into the square. He didn't need to tell them where to go or what to do next: they had seen what was to come several times before and knew what was expected, no-demanded of them. As the brawny ones tied the limp form of the foolish-troublesome one to a vertical post, their victim moaned from the physical agony caused by the torture. But his mind was clear. In spite of the pain, he had devised a plan for one more defiant act and was feigning unconsciousness in order to carry it out.

With difficulty the brawny ones tied the limp body to the post in a near standing position, and occasionally they would turn to the older robed man for approval of their efforts. Finally, they perceived a slight nod indicating approval. They began piling dry wood and straw around the feet of the limp form, stacking it higher and higher until it was at waist level. Then the old robed one placed the ancient scrolls that the foolish-troublesome one had been translating onto the highest part of the wood piled around the limp form. These scrolls contained words those in power did not ever want to become known outside their tight circle. The old robed one then turned to the brawny ones, one of whom was now holding high a burning torch. He extended his hand and the torch was passed to him. Holding the torch at arm's length, he began slowly pacing back and forth in front of the line of robed, hooded scribes.

Almost everyone who lived in the village had gathered to witness the coming spectacle; they knew they might be severely punished if they did not attend. There were those whose task it was to note who was present or absent and report to the powerful ones in charge; the no-shows sometimes were the ones next tied to a stake with flames licking around them. Among the crowd there were mixed feelings: fascination, revulsion and an ever-present fear that anyone could be accused of some trumped-up offense.

The old robed one continued pacing holding the flaming torch. Meanwhile, the brawny ones had momentarily disappeared through the doorway of a nearby building and soon returned, each carrying a large vat filled with oil used in lamps. They went directly to the wood stacked around the legs of the figure tied to the stake and began pouring the lamp oil onto the wood, emptying both vats. The older robed one abruptly stopped in front of one of the scribes, turned to face him, made a slight motion with his hand holding the torch and hissed, "Take it and set the fire."

His hand shaking almost uncontrollably, the scribe took the torch, stepped toward the pile of wood, leaned forward and tossed the flaming torch onto the oil-soaked funeral pyre. The pyre began to burn.

I could catch the scent of wood smoke, calling forth memories of scents which I remembered from when I camped in the forest as a boy. The flames crept higher. The figure tied to the stake began to stir. He raised his head, opened his eyes wide and stared, turning his head slightly left to right until he found the one for whom he had been looking—the older robed one—his stare widened and from his mouth came a sound that began as a low-pitched growl raising in tone until it ended in a high-pitched scream. All eyes in the entire crowd were riveted on the scribe tied to the stake. Then, as he began to feel the heat on his legs and waist, the scribe shouted out, the words he had translated, the words that those in power wanted to keep hidden forever. He screamed the words again, and again, and again; until, finally, the pain and the smoke overcame him; mercifully he lost consciousness as the smell of his burning flesh drifted throughout the crowd.

When the scribe began shouting the forbidden words, the older robed one abruptly stopped pacing and the color drained from his face. He knew he would be blamed for this failure to permanently silence the words the scribe had shouted to the crowd. He knew what his fate would be—and now it was he who was terrified. The scene faded from view, and I was relieved when it did.

Chapter 17
Oppression Through Religion

A new scene appeared, and I was on a vast, open expanse of sagebrush-covered plain. It was hot, dry and dusty; my throat felt parched and scratchy. As I glanced around, I saw a number of covered wagons, each drawn by a pair of oxen, spread out across the plain, all headed toward the silhouettes of mountains at the horizon. Old one let me know that the scene was in the mid-western United States. A strong wind blew the dust stirred up by the wagon armada into miniature tornados that dissolved into nothingness as they were blown downwind away from the slowly turning wagon wheels and the hooves of oxen. The wagons were not in a single-file procession. If they had been, the wagons in back would be smothered in the dust cloud.

The wagons were in a wavy line, crossways to their general direction of travel, which was westward. Some wagons were being driven by men, some by women; often one or two small children were seated beside the wagon driver. Many people walked along beside or in front of the wagons, men, women, and older children. Three young males walked side by side some distance ahead of the procession of wagons; they appeared to be young teenagers. I could hear them talking. The one who was tallest was speaking:

"I shore wisht Maw and my brothers hadn't took sick 'n up 'n died, back there, day afore yestiday. Buryin' 'em alongside the trail 'n then jist movin' on dint seem right a'tall. Now jist me 'n Paw is all whut's left uv muh fam'ly. I figger that there God person that I heered about from the preacher man done it. Thet there preacher man said thet God gits pissed off really easy ifn ya don't b'leave everythin thet he tells ya. I've listened to thet preacher man, but I jist cain't b'leave all thet stuff he says. So, I s'pose thet God fella is gittin' even with me by makin' Maw 'n my brothers take sick fer days 'n finely die like they done did."

The three strode on for a few moments, then the smallest of the three spoke up: "I don't b'leave all that stuff that the preacher man sez. A while ago, afore my real maw died, she tole me whut she b'leaved 'bout thet there God. She tole me thet God fella made us an' everthin' else, dirt, trees, all us people, animals, the sun, the moon, the stars, so it must be sumthin' really pow'ful. An' she said thet she b'leaved that ifn there really wuz thet God fella thet he don't git mad 'bout nuthin'—no how—no way—no siree! Only us people git mad wen stuff happens thet we don't like.

"My maw said thet all the preacher men she'd heered said thet if'n a person dint luv that God fella, thet he had made a place called Hell where when people died they would go to an' git burnt by fires and hurt tur'bul bad fer ever n' ever. So people purtended to b'leave everthin thet the preacher man tole 'em. Maw said thet dint make no sense to her. People wuz only sayin' thet they luv this God guy 'cause they are afeared of gittin' sent to thet there Hell place. It's like after my real maw died, my paw married up with another woman, an' I hafta tell her thet I luv her. Right after her an' my paw got married up, I dint know if I luved her or not. I guess I liked her okay, but I didn't luv her like I did my real maw. But this here new step-maw, she'd ask me ifn I luved her. Ifn I dint tell her I did, she'd whup me with a big, wide belt. So now I jist tell her I luv her so I won't git beat on no more. Seems to me it's the same way with thet there God. My real maw tole me thet she warn't certain thet there wuz a God, but if there wuz, he would be good 'n kind 'n nice 'n not make folks git sick 'n die, so I don't b'leave thet there God makes people git sick 'n die, stuff like thet jist happens."

Old One chuckled and spoke, "Now you know that you aren't the first person to figure out that I don't become angry. Many people throughout the ages have decided that I'm not vengeful or jealous or angry."

"What's next, Old One?" I asked.

Old One replied, "I have much more to show you, and it will be very painful for you to view. The reason I showed you scenes from the past was so you would see the origins of the lust for power and how it has been used in brutal and dishonest ways to gain and maintain power over others."

I waited for the next scenes to appear, which seemed like it was a long wait, and yet it wasn't. What Old One showed me next sickened me beyond my capability to describe. It was a journey through time in which I was shown some of the tyrants of the human race and the atrocities that either they or their assistants committed in order to force other human beings to obey them. They would justify their brutality by saying it was the only true religion and was would benefit the people they ruled; and that those who criticized or refused to follow its teachings must be punished – sometimes by death. Often, it was the political system that had to be obeyed, occasionally with religion mixed in. Any dissent was brutally dealt with, and religion or a political system gave the tyrants a reason to brutally suppress the slightest dissent.

In the earliest times, the killings and torture were simple: stoning to death, stabbing with sharp sticks, breaking skulls with rocks. Then, the killings became more sadistic and gruesome as the tyrants who held power took steps to prevent their people from challenging their power. They performed the killings where they would be witnessed by many people, who would be so fearful of angering those who had power that they would not dare to challenge the authorities and be subjected to the horrible cruel deaths that they had been forced to witness.

The crueler the torture and death the more effective it was in creating terror and thereby controlling masses of people. Those who broke the rules were skinned alive, pulled apart limb-from-limb by draft animals, burned, beheaded, killed by having their skin cut off little by little and given no water, or nailed to crosses and left to hang there and slowly suffer agonizing pain for days before death mercifully ended their agony. Horrific implements of torture were created to inflict pain and suffering and used in the name of various gods.

When I thought that even more cruel, inhumane acts could not be committed, Old One said, "Oh yes, it gets even worse! Those inhumane acts were intended to inflict agony upon the person themselves, but then the perpetrators of those heinous atrocities went on to inflict emotional anguish upon the loved ones of those being tortured and killed. Children would be tortured, raped, and mutilated while their parents were forced to watch; parents would be tortured, raped, mutilated and killed while their children were forced to watch. Unbelievable horrors were committed by those in power to cause such terror that no one would dare to challenge them in the slightest way for fear of being subjected to the same atrocities."

Old One showed me many unbelievably cruel rulers. Some of them had lived so long ago that their names were lost before recorded history. The most familiar names throughout history that Old One showed me were Attila the Hun, Genghis Khan, Torquemada, Ivan the Terrible, Idi Amin, Lenin, Stalin, Hideki Tojo, Hitler, Mao Tse-tung. These tyrannical and cruel rulers were responsible for policies that resulted in the cruel torture of many and the deaths of millions of human beings. However, it must always be remembered that these egotistical rulers seldom bloodied their own hands, but instead they set forth the policies and gave the orders that enabled their followers to perform the atrocities and murders.

And there were those who followed for different reasons. Some followed because they believed in the politics or religion of the leader, but this was usually not the case. Most followers feared that if they did otherwise they and their families would fall victim to the same atrocities or death. But a few of the followers cooperated with their cruel leaders either because it put them in a position of power over their victims or because they enjoyed inflicting terrible pain, watching people suffer, and seeing them die horrible deaths. None of the leaders could have come to power if there were not people to carry out their orders. Many people knew of the atrocities and murders but were afraid to raise their voices because they knew what the consequences would be if they spoke out.

My eyes well up with tears as I write this. I am thinking not only of the burning of the scribe but of all the other incidents of unspeakable cruelty throughout the history of humankind. Then, it's as if a comforting, soft, warm blanket cushions my feelings of sorrow and pain and the terrible knowledge of all the tragedies, brutalities, inequalities, and wrongs inflicted on humans by other humans. Old One eases my feelings of revulsion, helplessness and hopelessness. I'm no longer feeling overwhelmed by the suffering some humans have inflicted upon others. Old One has made me aware that most people don't want to be one of those in a position of power. They simply want to live their lives in peace as they choose, without causing harm to others. If an accident or disaster occurs, most people will pitch in to help the victims, often at great risk to themselves.

Old One spoke, "The most courageous people were those who knew what was taking place and did what small part they could, either by hiding those who were being persecuted or by helping them escape to someplace where they would be safe. They knew that they were placing themselves and their loved ones at extreme risk, yet they took that risk. Some of those brave people paid a terrible price.

"Listen to me. There are many people in your world who are performing heinous acts in your own time, and there are many more who would do so if they had the opportunity. Whenever the society over which a leader holds sway not only allows but orders its followers to commit atrocities in the name of a political system or a particular religion, that leader needs people to carry out brutal policies. Among the most recent are the Nazis, the regimes of Josef Stalin, Mao Zedong, Idi Amin, Kim-il-Sung, Kim Jong-il, Kim Jong-un and Saddam Hussein to name a few. People who blindly follow such a leader have little sense of self-worth. That's why strutting around in a uniform and possessing the power to brutalize transgressors provides them with a false sense of importance.

"Throughout the history of humanity, people have come to power who have committed unspeakable atrocities in the name of one religion or another. I know that most people who follow a particular religion simply want to live in peace; they may believe that other religions are wrong, but they are willing to tolerate them. Still, in any religion, there are fanatics that think they are pleasing me by trying to stamp out any belief other than theirs. In your own time, there have been instances of Hindus persecuting others who chose to celebrate a Christmas holiday even though they might not be Christians. Supposedly peaceful Buddhists are committing atrocities against Muslims. But the worst that is happening in your present time are the atrocities being committed by those fanatics who claim to be Muslim. Their atrocities include beheadings, murders of those they believe are apostates or "non-believers." They believe that they have the right to rape women and treat them as though they are the property of males without rights. There are those who join to commit these atrocities and claim that they want to fight and kill to avenge wrongs done to Muslims, but I know what is in their minds. They are people who have no love for themselves. Because they feel as though they are worthless, joining a group that encourages them to be brutal fills their need for power over others. And often another reason is because they are "given" girls and women to be their sex slaves. There is no fooling me; I know what is in the mind of every person and why they act as they do. But as I said the vast majority of Muslims as do those of the many other religions in your world, they sinply want to live their lives in peace.

I ask Old One, "Is there a Hell where people are punished for these atrocities?"

Old One answered, "You ask me about Hell, as you call it. Each one of you humans creates his or her own "Hell," and those people who have committed atrocities have much to fear. They will suffer the same agonies, both physical and emotional, they have inflicted upon every one of their fellow human beings. There is no escape!"

"Some followers are people who do so because they fear they will

142

be punished if they don't appear to support the regime in power. The leaders themselves need to believe that they are loved by the masses. They need constant reinforcement from followers telling them that they are extraordinary, superior beings. Of course, the followers are given special treatment by the leaders they pretend to revere.

"Most people who work in the field of law enforcement do so because they genuinely care about helping their fellow human beings, but a few want the power it allows them to wield. When they are confronted by people who don't immediately obey their orders, they react in a brutal way. Those who choose a career in law enforcement face an incredibly difficult task. Every time they are called to settle some sort of disturbance, they are risking their lives. They have no way of knowing in advance. The person or people they are confronting may be mentally ill, high on drugs or alcohol, or perhaps carrying a lethal weapon. Some criminals simply hate all police officers because they have no concern for anyone but themselves. The laws and the presence of law enforcement are the only things restraining them from harming others. Those who criticize law enforcement should have to experience what it is like to face such situations."

Old One added, "I know why people acted as they did. There is no fooling me. I know those who did cruel, atrocious things to their fellow humans only because they were terrified of what would happen to them or to their families if they didn't. I know of the people that did cruel atrocious things to their fellow humans because they wanted to and enjoyed doing so. I will tell you later how much it matters that every person feels good about himself or herself without being egotistical; but then egotism reflects a person's feeling of inferiority. Such people—the ones who crow about their own greatness—pretend to be more than they truly believe themselves to be. Often these are the people who choose to follow leaders that encourage or even urge them to be brutal in enforcing their leaders' policies. This gives them power over those people to whom, in the depths of their own minds, they feel inferior.

These are the people from which the likes of the Nazi Storm Troopers and others of that ilk were recruited. You must realize that such people are there in every society and would eagerly follow a leader that would allow, encourage and urge them to exert brutality toward their fellow human beings. There is no fooling me! I know what was and is in the hearts and minds of every human being. You are all a part of me. There is no hiding from me, no lying to me. I know!"

I spoke to Old One, "I sometimes wonder about myself. What would I have done if I had been brought up in the Nazi era and fed propaganda from a young impressionable age? Would I have been one of those committing atrocities?"

Old one replied, "There are many who think to themselves, 'I would never commit such atrocities. The people that did so were awful, evil people,' but every one of those people grew up and lived through a different set of circumstances. At any time in one's life each person is a summation of their experiences. I know what each one of you would have done if you had lived through the same situation. Some of you would have turned out to be good, caring, decent human beings; others would have done terrible things. Do not judge others by their actions. Leave that to me. I know how to take care of such things.

"You humans fight, kill and commit horrible atrocities upon each other over things I consider unimportant: what is my name, or who was my prophet, if there actually was any prophet. None of the many belief systems that are so important to some of you humans have it all figured out."

"How can the people of the Earth live in peace, Old One?" I ask.

Old One replies, "What must happen if humans are to ever live in peace with one another is for those of differing beliefs to sit around a table and discuss their differences. This could work if people agreed to limit the length of time that any one person may speak, with no interruptions, no anger, no shouting, no walking out, and no sneering when someone disagrees with another's beliefs. (You humans have such different ideas of what pleases me! Don't you realize how pleased I would be if you stopped fighting over me?) You know that this scenario is possible because if the person with whom you disagreed had the power to cause you or your loved ones great pain or death, you would control yourselves. So, it is possible that you can control your outbursts and anger, but you simply choose not to. You can't fool me, the "Old One," "God," or whatever you decide to name me. I know! I know that the reason most, though not all of you, refuse to engage in arguments without losing control is because you will be asked questions that you find it difficult or impossible to answer. You of differing opinions very often won't calmly and rationally discuss and work out your differences; and as a result, few problems are ever solved."

"You humans have achieved the capability of destroying the Earth. Some of your so-called 'holy books' talk about how I will someday destroy the Earth. I tell you now that I will never do that. If the Earth is destroyed, it will be because you humans do it. Stories were made up by people who were writing what are called 'holy books' about 'the end of the world' because they thought the writings would frighten people into living lives that didn't harm others, or make me angry enough to cause natural disasters, plagues, or invaders who attack and destroy, loot, enslave, rape, torture and kill. All the atrocities ever committed were done by people, not caused by me. The events you call 'natural disasters' are not caused by me. They simply happen, and it is all part of how you humans learn. Always remember this: I don't become angry!

"I have given you much to think about. Call me again after a while. There are questions you will want to ask me."

Chapter 18
Will The Human Race Survive?

What is it about flying that starts me thinking about the One who created the heavens and Earth? Needless to say, many of my conversations with Old One occurred when I was actually flying. On one occasion, I had an early morning flight from Seattle to Boise. The sky was totally cloudless over a big portion of the northwestern United States; a huge atmospheric high pressure system was centered over northeastern Oregon. I was ecstatic! Departure from Boeing Field was 3:30 a.m., and it was late June, just an hour before dawn. The flight passed over the northeast corner of Oregon and west of a spectacular mountain range called the Wallowas, several peaks of which were near 10,000 feet. I estimated that dawn and sunup would occur when I would be in perfect position to see awesome multiple sunrises. My guess was right on, and I was to see what I came to call, a "multiple sunrise." As I flew to the southeast, the sun appeared in the notch between peaks that were not as lofty as the highest peak, Mt. Sacajawea. Then as I flew on, the sun seemed to set behind Sacajawea, but reappeared as I passed it. I was in awe of the fantastic beauty, and my thoughts wandered to Old One, the cause of what I was witnessing and all else in our universe. Hey, Old One, I thought, are you there?

"You know that I'm always here," Old One responded. "What you have just done is the sort of 'worshipping' that pleases me and makes your life or anyone's life more worthwhile and enjoyable. You were awed by the scene that you saw. When you humans marvel at the wonders and beauty of all that I have caused to exist for intelligent life to perceive, I am better pleased than when you call me almighty and merciful. Pleasing me is so simple and easy. Be kind to one another and appreciate the wonder and beauty of living things, the Earth and the universe. Now, I know what you want to ask me, but I know that it makes more sense to you if you say it, so say it."

"Will the human race survive?" I asked Old One.

Old One paused a moment and then said, "You humans know that there is only one place for you to live, the planet Earth. Earth is finite in its size and resources. True, there are vast uninhabited areas where people could live, but why are they uninhabited? Because of climate extremes and access to resources vital for human existence, water being the most important. Other necessities for human survival include shelter, food, and energy. The greatest problem facing human survival is simply the growth of population. Earth's capacity to support the growing number of human beings is approaching its limit. Many of you humans know this but try to put it out of their minds. Others choose to deny it because it conflicts with what they have chosen to believe. Some societies are yet so primitive that it never enters the people's minds. All humans should remember the part of the reworked Fifth Commandment that says a child should not be created unless parents are certain, first, that they can make him or her feel truly wanted and, second, that they can provide the children with a decent life.

"You ask, 'Will the human race survive?' I won't answer that but consider the facts and then answer for yourself. The Earth is humanity's only home, and humans must care for it. Yet you humans are polluting the air and the water, throwing your garbage into the oceans, cutting vast forests, turning arable land into desert, and depleting the oceans of fish. And there are increasing numbers of you. How much longer can it continue? Many of you won't even trouble yourselves to refrain from littering when all it requires is a little self-discipline to dispose of trash properly. Your governments have created more than enough lethal weapons to destroy all life on your Earth. Now decide for yourself if humanity will survive.

I have given you much to think about, enough for now."

Chapter 19
Why I Fly, Scary Flight

Another conversation with Old One took place on a gorgeous evening in mid-May. The sky was not cloudless, but I saw nothing more threatening than some high stratus clouds, which were probably going to make for a gorgeous sunset. I had departed Spokane, landed at Wenatchee, Washington, picked up the freight from the couriers, and was in the air again within fifteen minutes, climbing toward twelve thousand feet as I prepared to fly over the Cascade Mountains westbound for Seattle. The sun was becoming golden, as it does when it descends in the sky nearing sunset. The route took me only a few miles from a rugged set of mountain peaks called the Stuarts, which glowed from the setting sun and lit up the snow clinging to their rocky crags. The vista was so awesome, I was filled with emotion at the wonder of it all.

My thoughts drifted back to when I was a four-year-old child. I was on the landing at the top of the stairs to the second floor of the old farmhouse where I lived with my family. That was the moment when I fell in love with airplanes and my dream of someday flying began. I don't remember what triggered it, but from that time on I was crazy about airplanes and wanted more than anything to become a pilot. I wonder why airplanes and the dream of becoming a pilot locked into my mind and has never left, after so many years. I have discussed this penchant for flying with other pilots, including some who spent their entire adult lives in the cockpit. Although a few of the others said that it had become "just a job," most of them told me they always loved flying and that it never felt like work. I felt the same way, and that job flying small airplanes carrying cargo was the only time in my life when I couldn't wait to get to work.

Simply watching the ground pass below fascinated me. There were farm fields laid out in neat rectangles or in irrigation circles. On a clear, dark night, the picture of the ground that I saw below was like having a map laid out beneath me. Towns and cities sparkled with light, and the roads that joined them stood out like connecting lines. A clear moonlit night was especially beautiful, particularly when the ground below was covered with snow and reflecting the moonlight.

And there were times when I flew among clouds. Flying in solid clouds was not that much fun. In daylight hours, it was like flying in a bucket of milk. In cloud during nighttime all that is visible is the glow of the instruments, with the red wingtip light glowing on the left, the green on the right, and the flashing strobes lighting up the surrounding cloud.

My favorite flying times were when I was among small- to medium-sized cumulus clouds, often called "fair weather Qs." I loved flying through the holes and the canyons, entering a cloud and wondering what the "cloudscape" would look like when I popped out the other side. It always made me recall the beautiful song written by Joni Mitchell, "Both Sides Now." The opening lines of the lyrics, "Rows and flows of angel hair/and ice-cream castles in the air / and feather canyons everywhere," describe flying among clouds perfectly, and I found it to be almost mesmerizing.

Flying in and out of clouds, or flying on a cloudless, moonless night at ten thousand feet or higher, where the air is clear, always brought my thoughts to Old One, the supreme Creator of all I saw. From the cockpit the panorama was as though there was an artist with a palette of myriad colors, an infinite supply of brushes varying in widths and textures, and an imagination extending to infinity. On a clear moonless night, a vast expanse of stars would appear before me, and it was as if a perfectly transparent window opened, giving me a glimpse into eternity.

It never grew old for me, and the memories of what I saw are still vivid. Those flying experiences bought me closer to Old One, the divine artist who created all this splendor and made me more certain of Its existence. The boundless sky serves as a studio where Old One creates a never-ending series of masterpieces.

Flying in dry snow was out of this world. When the strobes flashed, snowflakes appeared to be frozen in place at the wingtips like a collection of tiny stars. If the airplane was equipped with a landing light in the nose, turning it on while flying in snow was like the scene from the movie 2001: A Space Odyssey, with the snowflakes rushing toward you as streaks. The dry snow brushing the airplane's exterior would create static electrical charges, causing miniature lightning flashes that would randomly jump around on the windshield inside the cockpit. Holding my hand close to the windshield, I could feel the slight tingle of electricity flowing from my fingertips and see blue miniature lightning arcs jumping to the windshield. Often a glowing ring of Saint Elmo's fire would appear as the circular arc traced by the propeller tips.

Only on one occasion did I encounter a situation that caused me to wonder if I would survive—and to question why I continued to fly. It was mid-January. My flight that evening was a return to Seattle from Spokane with a stop in Wenatchee. The weather check forecast winds of eighty knots at 12,000 feet almost directly on the nose for the entire flight. The Wenatchee-Seattle leg required a 12,000-foot cruise altitude, so ground speed would be only about eighty knots. The time for that leg would be nearly one hour for the approximately seventy-five-mile leg, and with winds like that over the mountains there would likely be severe turbulence. I departed Spokane and flew the leg to Wenatchee at 6,000 feet, where opposing wind was much less. That leg was unremarkable.

Couriers were waiting when I arrived at Wenatchee, and I was back in the air and climbing to 12,000 within fifteen minutes under starry skies. I was amazed because there was no turbulence. The sky above was clear. All went well except for the reduced ground speed, due to the wind on the nose. At about forty-five miles from Seattle, I tuned in to the Boeing Field weather and heard the words, "ceiling 4,000, visibility ten miles, light surface winds, freezing level 5,000." I remember thinking, Great, if I pick up ice in the descent, it'll be gone long before landing. Once the temperature is freezing or above, ice is shed very rapidly. No sweat, I thought. Things are looking good.

At forty miles from Seattle, the controller's voice crackled in my headset: "Aeroflight 660, descend to 10,000." I saw no reason to refuse the controller's instruction. There were only ten miles more of significant mountains. I would have more than adequate mountaintop clearance, so I lowered the nose.

At 11,800 feet I entered the cloud tops and all hell broke loose. I immediately encountered severe turbulence, and ice began rapidly piling up on the windshield and wings. At 11,500 feet, I called the controller and requested to go back to 12,000 feet because of the ice and turbulence. I was given clearance back to 12,000, but the airplane would not climb. In less than one minute, enough ice had piled onto the airplane that it was difficult to maintain control, and I could neither climb nor hold altitude. I was in an involuntary gradual descent because of the ice. I informed the controller of the situation and was cleared to whatever altitude I needed, down to 8,000 feet.

Now a few words about the airplanes that were in the fleet. It was a motley collection of Cessna 172s, 402s, a Cessna 421, several Piper Senecas, and two Piper Chieftains. All of the planes were of various vintage, mainly manufactured in the 1970s, older than most of the pilots who were using this flight experience to build hours before moving up to regional airlines. The Cessna 402s were all quite similar, but they differed in their radios and locations of switches for lights, heater and other equipment. All had a number of switches and push-pull circuit breakers on the left side of the cockpit where an armrest would be in a car. The Cessna 402 that I was flying was the only one without a push-pull circuit breaker for the radios. It had a combination switch and circuit breaker, which I didn't notice. The radio power switch was one of four, positioned side-by-side. The switch closest to the sidewall was for the cabin heater and the avionics/radio switch was farthest from the side wall closest to the pilot's left. I don't recall what the two switches between the heater switch and radio switch controlled.

I wasn't panicked, but I sure as hell was uptight as I wrestled with the turbulence, saw more ice accumulating on the wings, heard chunks of ice flung off the propellers and occasionally hitting the fuselage, and watched the altimeter slowly unwind. This was the only time in all my flying that I asked Old One, "Am I going to make it through this?" Old One chuckled and said, "Just fly the airplane." I asked myself why I was doing this job when I didn't have to, but I knew that when the schedule showed that I was assigned a flight I would do it again.

The heater in that airplane didn't maintain a comfortable temperature particularly well; it was either too hot or too cold. Because of the tense situation and the heat in the cockpit, I was sweating and decided to turn off the heater switch against the side wall. A few minutes passed. I was still very intent on maintaining control, though I was still slowly losing altitude. Then I realized I haven't heard any radio conversations. I knew I should be hearing Seattle Center talking to me or to some other flights. I scanned the radio panels.

The radios were of old vintage before LED displays and had numbers that rotated like odometer digits in a car, with cockpit lighting to illuminate them. But one of radio displays did have LEDs that showed frequency and DME, or Distance Measuring Equipment. DME is the acronym for which I had tuned into the Seattle VOR navigational frequency. It should have been showing a readout of thirty to thirty-five miles, but it was dark. I was thinking, No readout! Holy shit! No wonder I hadn't heard any radio chatter. My radios were all dead. I grabbed my flashlight and started looking for a push/pull circuit breaker for the radios, but I couldn't find one. The appearance of the radio power combination switch and breaker was hardly different from a non-combination switch. In the dimly lit cockpit, I didn't notice the difference.

Fortunately, I had a handheld combination communication/ navigation set in my flight bag. I got it out, turned it on and tuned to the frequency for Seattle Center, which was calling me. I responded, but the handheld transmit power was not great enough for them to hear my response. They asked a Delta Airlines flight that was in my vicinity to try to contact me, but that didn't work. After a few more attempts to contact me, they said, "Aeroflight 660, if you hear this turn to heading 270." I turned to that heading, and after maybe thirty seconds, they knew that I could hear them and that they could assign headings and altitudes to get me safely to about 4,000 feet, the base of the cloud cover where the turbulence subsided.

I continued the descent, and upon reaching the freezing level at about 5,000 feet, the ice on the wings and windscreen began rapidly falling away. The familiar light patterns of Issaquah, Bellevue and Seattle appeared when I broke out of the bottom of the cloud layer, and I passed over Bellevue at about 2,000 feet while heading for the west end of the I-90 floating bridge. I flashed my landing lights when I knew Boeing Tower could see me, and they gave me a green light to land.

I landed, taxied into base, shut down engines, completed the shutdown checklist, unloaded the freight, finished the necessary paperwork and went into the office. The company had recently hired on a new general manager, the previous one having moved on to a major airline pilot job. The new guy was great: he was all business but also had an easy manner about him and a great sense of humor. He had been monitoring my situation on the office radio receiver, and we talked about the "interesting" flight that I had managed to survive. Then he sent a maintenance person to the airplane to check out the radios. The company had its own frequency, and the maintenance person's voice came over the radio saying, "This is number one. How do you hear?" Without hesitation the General Manager responded, "Can't hear a thing. Try number two." Again, I heard the voice of the maintenance person say, "Number two. How do you hear?" The General Manager replied, "Can't hear a thing. Have to send it to the radio shop tomorrow."

Well, I had egg on my face, big time! I went out to the airplane with my flashlight and looked at the radio power switch. There it was. A combination switch/circuit-breaker. I figured out what must have happened. When I turned off the heater, I must have inadvertently

154

bumped the radio switch off and didn't think to check its position. I felt pretty stupid!

There's a humorous saying among airplane pilots: There are two kinds of landings, good ones and great ones. Landings that are merely good the pilot can walk away from the airplane; whereas after a great landing the airplane can be flown again.

Chapter 20
Does God Exist?

I was flying among the clouds again and in that mystical state of mind that preceded conversations with Old One. Marveling at the beauty all around me, I thought again of the One who created humans to marvel at all the creation. Then, Old One was with me, putting thoughts into my mind.

"Many of you humans make problems for yourselves because of what you call "ego." Throughout your history there have been many prominent people who, because of the position they held and their inflated opinion of themselves, made statements that were later proven totally wrong. Consider these examples from the past:

The Earth is flat, so any ship sailing to the horizon will fall off into the unknown.

The sun and stars revolve around the Earth.

Nothing will replace whale oil as a source of fuel for heating and lighting homes.

Passengers riding on trains that go faster than a horse can run will die from asphyxiation.

The theory that things exist that are so small the human eye cannot see them and are the cause of infection and disease is utterly ridiculous.

Electricity is a passing fad of no possible use.

Creating light from electricity is impossible.

Steamships and submarines will never exist anywhere other than in the imagination.

Automobiles are a passing fad and will never replace the horse.

Tanks will never replace horse-mounted cavalry.

Man will never create a 'flying machine.'

Airplane travel will never replace train travel.

It is impossible to ever build an airplane capable of flying across an ocean.

Airplanes will never fly faster than the speed of sound.

Man will never go into space, much less travel to the moon.

A white light-emitting diode is impossible.

Smoking tobacco does not cause cancer.

The Atomic Theory is nonsense.

"Business leaders in high positions stated there was too small a market for radio, telephone, television, copying machines, or computers, and on and on, with people making pronouncements because of their egos. Many of those ideas or predictions, which were said to be impossible, have become commonplace. As for those ideas that haven't yet become reality: we don't know how to overcome the obstacles at this time. That's all that needs be said.

"I repeat. All that anyone should ever say is that humans do not know how to accomplish something at the time the statement is made. New knowledge may prove possible those technologies that were previously thought to be impossible. Making a statement that something is impossible implies that the speaker knows all there is to know. Sometimes people make such statements to gain a business advantage or to maintain a position of power over people.

"At the time you are writing this, scientists state that the speed of light cannot be exceeded. What they should say is that, with our present level of knowledge, it appears that the speed of light cannot be reached or exceeded."

"Did you cause the universe to have this apparent speed limit?" I asked Old One.

"Yep, I built that into how I constructed your universe. And why do you suppose that I did that? There may be forms of life in the universe that you humans cannot even imagine. If you encountered them, you might wage war on them. They might be of a form that you would find repulsive or threatening. Think of the strange life forms that have been discovered on your Earth, existing where the existence of life was considered impossible; an example being the creatures that thrive near fumaroles at great depths in the seas, in the dark and in extreme temperatures.

"Many of you people choose not to live in harmony with others of different skin color, ethnicity, political or religious beliefs. How would you humans cope with intelligent, alien beings that bear no resemblance to your human form? It all comes down to what I talk about later: feeling good about oneself. Loving yourself. Loving yourself, without being egotistical, matters very much because when people accept themselves for what they perceive themselves to be, they don't feel threatened by other people of different appearances or beliefs.

"Regarding the secrets of the universe in which you exist, you humans have barely scratched the surface. And don't forget about the people who solved problems that were considered impossible. Humankind would have made little progress if there had not been some people that dreamed and attempted what was considered impossible, and sometimes, they succeeded. Such people often were often considered by others of their time as foolish, troublesome, and blasphemous. Sometimes those in power felt so threatened by those innovators that they felt compelled to imprison them or kill them. Your Thomas Edison's response to a reporter who interviewed him during the time he was working on the development of the electric, incandescent light bulb and had been unsuccessful after many failures. The reporter asked him if he should give up trying after failing so many times. Edison's reply was that he hadn't had any 'failures.' He had proven many ways that didn't work, he wouldn't need to try those again..

"There have been countless numbers of people who have contributed to the advancement of human-kind since the time I showed you when your primitive ancestors still lived in caves and the 'foolish-troublesome' one who had learned how to start a fire. There have been explorers who wanted to see what was on the other side of mountains, across a river or over the horizon. There have been those who were fascinated by the phenomena of nature and strove to gain understanding. There have been those who were intrigued by human behavior and studied it, then wrote of their findings, which sometimes shed light on the reasons for human failures and problems."

"Why do some people make statements about things that are impossible to prove?" I asked Old One.

Old One Answered, "Think back to our first conversation. Remember I said that some people feel that it is 'important to be important'; such people make statements which cannot be proven because they gain a feeling of 'importance.' There have been many very intelligent people who made statements that various things were impossible to achieve, yet many of those things are now commonplace. Many of these same people claim that there is no God, that I do not exist. Haven't any of them thought that a Creator of the universe could have arranged things such that Its existence could not be proved or disproved? Some of you humans have such an over-sized ego! How many phenomena exist of which you humans have not yet even imagined? For you humans there are so many unknowns. Yet some of you, who are very intelligent, refuse to even admit that it is possible for a Creator to exist. They state that they believe that there is no God, no Creator." Old One paused chuckled. Then continued saying, "But I know that way down in their deepest thoughts, which they try their hardest to keep from their consciousness, they are unsure that I don't exist, and they don't want to admit it to themselves and certainly never to another person. Now, I ask all you people who are so certain that I don't exist: where is the proof? You are all so wrapped up in proving things, and you are correct in much of what you have learned about nature. But can any of your super-smart people prove that I don't exist? No, they can't. No one can. I made things that way."

"I find myself laughing, Old One," I said. "Members of my own family have read some of what I have written and think I am off my rocker because I say that you and I have (maybe) 'talked via thoughts.'"

"I know that," Old One replied with a chuckle, "and that's all right.

They are different from you because they have travelled a different journey through life. In their journey through life, they haven't experienced what you have experienced—and that allowed you to think that I just possibly might exist and would communicate with you if you asked. Down within their deepest thoughts, they are reluctant to ask that I communicate with them and would feel foolish doing so. Whatever their reason is, I know and understand it—and it doesn't matter to me. Many of you humans believe or claim to believe the religious beliefs you were taught from the time you were children; and many cases it instilled a fear of me that often remains throughout life. The manner in which you communicate with me conflicts with what they were brought up to believe. I'll tell you more another time. You're about to hear from Seattle Center."

The air traffic controller's voice crackled in my headset, "Aeroflight 660: descend to 4,000. Contact approach on one-one-niner-point-two."

Chapter 21
An Infinite Universe?

I was sitting on a bench, watching a river flow by. "Mom and pop" mallard duck drifted down river with the current. After a cooler than normal spring, the day was delightfully warm. The sky was deep blue with puffy white clouds moving to the east. The many cottonwood trees along the riverbank were producing billions of their fuzzy seeds, as they do in springtime. Scattered here and there were piles of the fuzzy seeds, some heaped a couple of inches deep. I was watching a fuzzy cottonwood seed float past me when I also noticed a flying insect so tiny that I could barely see it.

My thoughts focused on the cottonwood seed, the insect and the miracle contained in each. Within the tiny cottonwood fuzzy seed was the blueprint necessary for it to sprout, grow, and after many years become a huge, magnificent tree around one hundred feet tall. The tiny insect had a brain capable of controlling its minuscule body, controlling the wing motions that enabled it to fly, seek a mate, and make countless decisions affecting its existence. Old One, who caused all I was observing, must be far beyond our ability as humans to comprehend. I always feel humbled when I think of Old One.

Then Old One entered my mind with a chuckle and said, "There you go 'worshiping' me again in the manner that pleases me the most. Don't kneel to worship me; stand, look with eyes wide open, appreciate and marvel at my creations, and treat one another with kindness and respect. I say again that it means nothing to me when people 'pray' and begin their ritual by kneeling and clasping hands, closing their eyes and saying, 'almighty and most merciful God.' They think that I need my ego boosted as many humans do, so they tell me how great I am. Well, I know that most of them don't really mean it. Most people feel that they are pleasing me by doing this, and I am in no way offended by their doing so; I am only saying that it is unnecessary. Now, ask me your question."

"Is the universe infinite?" I asked Old One.

"Hey, that's a really good question," Old One answered. "I'll give you some words on that topic that will give you much to mull over. What does 'infinite' mean when it's used to describe the universe? You humans define the word 'infinite' as 'endless'; thus, infinite space relative to the universe means that it goes on forever. There is no boundary, no edge, no limit. Okay, let's say I did create an infinite universe. Wouldn't that mean that if a person could travel through the universe, he or she would forever see that there were more galaxies and stars, stars which would have planets circling them, intelligent life living on the planets? If so, wouldn't that also mean that there is an infinite quantity of the stuff that you humans have thus far discovered—what you call atoms—of which you humans think everything is made?

"So, what is a human being—a person, an individual? Is each person nothing more than a unique combination of atoms? If so, then there must be an infinite number of each human because each human is not made of an infinite number of atoms. Each human is made of a large number of atoms, but still not an infinite number. Then this means that there is an infinite number of each unique combination of atoms, which means that there is an infinite number of unique human beings. But then, maybe there is something else in each human being that makes each one unique—something that your scientists haven't discovered. Perhaps I have created the universe and intelligent life in such a way that some questions will never be answered. How's that for an answer to your question? That's a lot for you humans to think about. I'll be back another time."

I watched the fuzzy cottonwood seeds float by, and the tiny insects flitting frantically around on whatever mission their miniscule brains directed them—and I was still in awe thinking of the intelligence that caused it all: Old One.

Chapter 22
Self-Confidence, Prayer, Belonging

I was in the woods, down the steep hillside on the lower part of the five-acre property behind the house that I had built. The property was mostly forested with Douglas fir, hemlock, cedar, and a few alders, vine maple and big leaf maple. It was quiet, except for the rushing sound of wind in the trees. A large fir near the edge of the backyard had died of a root-rot disease that was killing fir trees. The dead fir was probably 125 feet tall, and if it had blown over in a wind storm, it might have guillotined the house. With a neighbor's help, who had once been a logger, the fir was felled, nicely down the hill, then limbed and yarded down the hill to a relatively level spot, where I bucked it up into fireplace lengths. I got lots of healthy exercise, so I called cutting and splitting wood "my gym."

On that day, the job at hand was splitting the short fireplace lengths. I loved everything about doing that hard work: the smells of the wood, even the achy muscles that resulted from working hard for two or three hours. I was sitting on an upended wood block, catching my breath after splitting a really tough, crazy grained block that had tried its damnedest to resist splitting. I counted the number of sledge-hammer blows to the wedge. It had taken twenty-eight hits before the block of wood gave up and separated. I was pleased at what I had accomplished as I glanced at the sizeable pile of wood that I had split. I was also grateful that I could work that hard, being then in my mid-seventies. And in those peaceful forest surroundings, I called up Old One. I had become comfortable conversing with Old One, and now when I had a question and was ready to receive an answer, a response would usually be forthcoming—even though sometimes Old One told me to figure it out for myself.

Old One said, "What is the subject this time?"

"Old One," I said, "is it important and good for people to love themselves?"

Old One answered: "There is a huge difference between loving yourself—feeling good about yourself and accepting yourself—and being egotistical. Egotistical people do not love themselves and lack self-confidence. If people truly feel good about themselves, they don't need to boast about their accomplishments. Consider how two different people tell of an accomplishment. When people boast, it comes across as them telling of some accomplishment, implying that they are the only person who could ever successfully complete such an impossibly difficult task. People who feel good about themselves do not need to crow about what they have accomplished, but they still can be pleased that they have overcome some obstacle. They can proudly but humbly tell others of their accomplishment. There are those who are so lacking in self-esteem that they compensate by behaving in an obnoxiously arrogant manner, with the result that they drive people away and then cannot understand why people try to avoid them.

"When people don't love themselves, don't feel good about themselves and lack self-confidence, often they are afraid to attempt to improve their situation in life. They are afraid that if they attempt something that appears difficult to them they will fail. They are beaten without even trying. They think something they would like to do is beyond their capability.

Often acquaintances will discourage them from trying to reach a goal, and they may say that someone is acting 'uppity.' Friends do this often out of jealousy; they don't want someone to achieve more than they have. Families fear that they may lose a member to a different social class."

I said, "I have experienced that sort of treatment in my own life: people putting me down when I mentioned getting more education or hoping to get into a particular career. I also did some of that thing of not trying hard enough at some things because I thought I would fail."

Old One switched gears and said, "As I have said before, I often hear people saying, 'almighty and most merciful God,' followed by the speaker asking me to do something. I am not offended when people say those flowery words, but it is not necessary. I know what I am and, to put it in human words, 'I feel good about myself.' People say those words when they 'pray' to me because they feel that I need to be flattered like many of the powerful people on Earth. They think I will be offended or angry and will cause terrible things to happen unless they 'butter me up" and that if they tell me how great I am, I will answer their prayers or not be angry with them and punish them in some merciless way."

"Do you answer prayers, Old One?" I asked.

Old One said, "I won't answer that other than to say, maybe I do, maybe I don't," and with a slight chuckle went on. "I might tweak things now and then. Many people gain much comfort and cause no harm to anyone by asking me—'praying' to me—to do certain things and by believing that I do them.

"I don't want to take that comforting thought away from them by saying I don't. As I said, maybe I tweak things sometimes. Often, people pray for things that are truly unselfish, such as asking for me to heal a sick or injured loved one, or for there to be peace on Earth. I will say, however, that if what a person prays for is only for selfish purposes, that prayer will certainly not be answered.

"People sometimes pray for things to happen that they could make happen themselves if they would only try. People pray for outcomes that are nice but don't really matter at all, such as results of various sorts of contests or sporting events, the outcomes of which are nice but so utterly unimportant. People rooting for their chosen athletic teams sometimes pray for the outcome that they want; so, what I am supposed to do? Should I answer the prayers of those who pray the hardest, the ones asking for a particular outcome in the greatest number, or the ones who flatter me with words like 'almighty' and 'merciful'? Winning games is nice but not with something that really matters. People hoot and holler, and if their team comes out in first place yell, 'We're number one!' But they didn't do anything to deserve being number one, other than watching other people play a game.

"There are those of you who work hard and thereby become very wealthy. It is just fine with me for people to gain wealth, as long as it is achieved through diligent effort and without being dishonest. Sometimes people become wealthy through an inheritance, or they just get lucky. No matter how people attain wealth, if they are worthy of it, they will retain it and perhaps cause it to grow; those who are not worthy will lose it. There are people for whom there is never enough. This 'big ego' thing comes into play, and they flaunt their wealth. They are continually competing against other wealthy people whom they fear may have done better than they have. They are never satisfied with what they have earned and always want still more. Then there are those who simply keep doing something that they love and that they find fulfilling; if it increases their wealth and is done without harming other people, good, but if not, that's all right too. Often, these people who have done well make very generous gifts of their wealth to worthy causes. Good for them!

"Many people feel a need to belong, to associate themselves with a group, either ethnic, religious, or social, in their struggle to gain and maintain some sense of self-worth and inclusion. They pretend to believe as others in their chosen group do, but I know what they truly believe. If pretending to believe the same doctrine as their chosen group does brings them happiness, without causing other people harm in any way, it is all okay with me.

"Enough for now," Old One said. "Call for me anytime; if I know it's the right time for you to talk, I'll answer. Remember, for me there is no time. I know it all, past, present, future."

Chapter 23
Altruism

I was browsing through a calendar at nearly midnight, marveling at what to me were awe-inspiring pictures. I had saved that calendar for several years and would occasionally pick it up and page through. There were twelve pictures of spectacular Hubble Space Telescope images. I was overwhelmed not only by the unbelievable beauty, but also by distances of space and time so vast that they are almost beyond comprehension. The telescope captured events that had occurred long before Earth was even formed and whose light was only then reaching the Hubble Telescope, which made possible the pictures that I was viewing. To think that there is a Creator of all this, with whom I can converse, fills me with emotion and wonder beyond description!

Old One, I thought, how magnificent it all is!

"There you go again. Worshipping me in a way that pleases me," Old One said. "Now, what shall we talk about this time?"

"Please, let's discuss how best to help other people?" I asked Old One.

Old One answered, "Good thought. Here goes! There are two kinds of people who seek help: those who genuinely need help and those who choose to make little or no effort to help themselves and make excuses for their difficult circumstances and lack of effort. To say it briefly, there are those that can't help themselves and those who won't help themselves. But they can't fool me. I know who is truly needy, and who does not put forth effort to improve their situation. Those who cannot help themselves deserve help and should be helped; such people usually don't receive all the help they need and should get because of those who choose not to make an effort to improve their situation and thereby stretch thin the resources available for help. Then there are those who either are of little means or are already receiving help, and who spend what they have or receive foolishly. Remember how I expanded about

Commandment Eight and the ways there are to steal? Some people are born into poverty, experience neglect and perhaps abuse, but still work hard, struggle, grasp every opportunity, and ascend out of seemingly impossible circumstances and achieve success. They had the courage to try to better their situation.

"When it comes to helping others, people do so for different reasons. Those people who help and do so quietly without boasting about what they are doing, simply because it gives them a good feeling inside, are helping for the right reason. There is nothing wrong with feeling good about oneself and gaining satisfaction from doing good deeds or simply being kind.

"Then there are those who help others, but always let it be known what they are doing. Put simply, they boast about their good works. It gives them a feeling of being 'better than' those they are helping. There also are those who make a big show of how they want to help the less fortunate. They provide an excuse for those being helped to do little or nothing to help themselves. Among these people are the politicians whose re-election depends upon getting the votes they need from those people they profess to care about; but all they truly care about is retaining their position. They actually care little for those they are helping; often within their own minds they hold them in contempt. They care not at all that by creating a class of people that are dependent upon them for largesse, they are actually destroying people's lives by making them dependent rather than capable. There is no fooling me. I know what is in every person's mind and why they choose to act as they do.

"Then there are those who come into unearned wealth through happenstance or inheritance. Many of these people spend their new-found wealth foolishly and become poor again in a short time. If all the wealth on Earth were divided equally among all people, within a relatively short time, it would go back close to the way it was before the redistribution took place because so many people would not manage it wisely; they would spend it unimportant and foolish things."

I asked, "I don't know if I made up this phrase, or if I heard or read it sometime. The phrase is: 'The less responsibility demanded from people, the less responsible they will be.' Do you agree with this, Old One?"

Old One replied without hesitation, "You have heard or known of children whose parents overindulged them and who, therefore, never became responsible adults; that answers your question doesn't it? No person truly feels worthwhile unless they are accomplishing something through their own efforts. I also know how to handle what you humans see as inequality. Some of you don't think that there should be any 'inequality.' Well, you are not all equal, no matter that some of you believe you are and want it to be so. You are not born equal. Each one of you is a unique individual; no two people are even close to being alike. Each of you from birth starts out on the path of life with his or her own collection of gifts or impediments; mental, physical or situational. What a person does with those gifts and how they cope with and manage difficult circumstances depends upon the makeup of the individual. Some people will manage to overcome very difficult or unfortunate circumstances; other people will not make the most of excellent circumstances.

"And there are people who provide for family members who are addicted to drugs or alcohol or are unwilling to exert the effort necessary to care for themselves. These providers are doing so primarily to minimize criticism of themselves and their family. By doing so, these providers are enabling the irresponsible individual to continue to avoid taking steps to improve their situation. Giving to people who panhandle or stand by a stoplight showing a sign describing a desperate situation is also enabling because the money you give will likely be spent to support an addiction. People can get help through many governmental or charitable organizations; donations to such entities is the best way to help. That's enough for you to think about until we talk next time."

Chapter 24
Human Freedom

I was mowing my lawn, walking behind a power lawn mower. I had noticed other times that certain sounds—the rushing sound of a river, the whispering of wind in the limbs of trees, the low rumble of airplane engines while flying or of a power mower while mowing—would lull my mind into a state of thoughtfulness during which I would enter an almost dreamlike semi-consciousness. I think I have heard that sort of noise referred to as "white noise," although "white noise," I believe, is totally random whereas engine noise definitely has a repetitive frequency associated with it. In any event, I could manage to mow and yet think of Old One and the questions that I had yet to ask.

And Old One entered my mind and told me to ask the question that was drifting to the forefront of my thoughts.

So, I asked my wordless question, "Should people be free?"

Old One replied, "Certainly they should be free, and I will say much about why this is so. If people are not truly free, then it is never known to others what they truly think and believe. I know, but no other person on Earth truly knows. The way things are now on your planet, there are divisions which you call 'countries.' In each of these countries some form of social order and authority which you call 'government' has been established and in some countries the governments decree that a particular belief system, or 'religion,' must be followed.

"Now if I were one to be insulted, any government or social system that lays down rules requiring the inhabitants to follow a certain religion would be a huge insult to me. It is, however, impossible to insult me. I know what I am; I don't need you humans to say nice things about me, so I will feel good about myself, and if people don't believe that I exist and state so publicly or within their own thoughts, I could care less. I know that most people have doubts about my existence but are afraid to admit it because they fear that I will punish them, or that their church,

175

family, or community might reject them.

"Neither the government nor any individual on Earth knows what another person is truly thinking. If there are punishments for not following the belief system decreed by law, people will pretend to believe. This is utterly ridiculous because I, the Old One, know what every person believes. People who bow or kneel before me and call me 'Almighty and Most Merciful God' cannot possibly believe all that they claim to believe about me. If I am as 'great and all powerful,' as they say I am, then they are saying that I must know what they are thinking. I do know what every human being is thinking, and I know that if people were not compelled by threats of severe punishments to pretend they believe in a state religion, most people would not pretend to believe. They would desert by the millions.

"This is the reason that the 'leaders' want to control what their people see, hear or read. The 'leaders' would lose their lofty position, which is why they are afraid of words. As I said, if I were one to be insulted, then forcing people to pretend to follow a certain religion concerning me would certainly make me feel insulted.

"Coercion, forcing people to pretend that they follow a certain belief system, applies not only to a religion dictated by government, but also to smaller social groups. As I said before, many people feel the need to be part of some social group whose members profess to share a common belief. If members of that group question the belief system, they are sometimes banished from belonging, which may be very emotionally painful; and so people will pretend to believe in what one of your writers referred to as 'group think.'

"Children, often much too young to understand what they are being taught, will assure their parents that they believe what their mothers or fathers teach them. Children often do this out of fear that their parents will be angry or will shame them if they question what they were being taught. I know that this happened to you when you were a child and was one of the reasons that you have been trying to arrive at a belief of what

I am like.

"People not being free to believe as they choose and state their beliefs, political or religious, openly, without any fear of punishment results in many of your Earth's problems. There have been people who have been tortured or killed for refusing to state that their religion is the wrong one and agreeing to follow a different belief. To anyone finding themselves in that situation: I say, tell them what they want to hear; save your life. Remember, I don't become angry. I know what is in everyone's mind: what they are thinking and what they truly believe. If I am so 'kind and merciful,' as I am so often told I am, does it make sense that I would want a person to be tortured or killed rather than utter a statement that they don't actually believe? Again, say whatever they want to hear to save your life or end the torture. And always remember—I don't get angry or offended!

"Finally, no one should ever be enslaved! Every human being must be free! People who enslave others because they have the power to do so or because they believe they have a right to, will learn what it is like to be a slave, and men who enslave women in any manner will experience the pain and misery they have inflicted. Now, go on with mowing your lawn. I always know when you have another question."

I finished mowing my lawn while mulling over what Old One had just told me.

Chapter 25
Hell? What Is It?

I was propped up against a tree on a grassy bank beside a river filled almost to overflowing its banks. It was springtime and the weather had warmed somewhat, causing faster than usual snowmelt in the mountains. The sound of the river rushing downstream lulled my senses into a dreamlike state: an utterly random, peaceful, gentle, soughing sound, which resulted in my mind beginning to drift through the volumes of thoughts collected through more than eight decades of life. A friend with whom I had shared office space many years ago had a saying that I found to be somewhat descriptive of me and which I have never forgotten. He called a situation such as I was experiencing "sitting and watching the snails whiz by."

A treasured memory of my childhood is of being in a forested part of my parents' property in the Adirondack area of upstate New York, lying on my back on a soft bed of thick green moss. It was late morning on a beautiful, pleasantly warm, summer day. A gentle breeze blowing through the long needles of the white pine trees surrounding my mossy cushion made a soft, sighing sound. My head cushioned by the soft moss, I gazed straight up toward the bright blue sky and watched through gaps in the tree branches as yellow-white clouds drifted by, wafted along by the wind.

Feeling as if I were suspended in a sort of never-never time, I wondered if there was something that caused everything to exist. I had heard the word "God" and was told that God made the Earth and everything else, but also that if people didn't believe what they were told, God would get mad and punish them by sending them to a terrible place called Hell, where they would be burned and suffer forever. I knew that down deep I didn't really believe, and I was afraid that God was out to get me because I wasn't sure. I had doubts, but I still wondered.

As I was remembering my childhood speculations about God, Old

One suddenly spoke up: "I was there with you then as I am now. You have learned much in the intervening years. The most important thing you have learned is not to fear me and not to be afraid to admit that you are still unsure if I exist. Now, I'll talk about that Hell place that you were told of and made to fear when you were but a child."

So, I asked Old One, "Is there a Hell punishment for the 'sins' that people commit? Is Hell, as humans have depicted it, a place where people are punished for wrongs they have committed?"

Old One chuckled and paused for a moment before replying. "In times long past people concocted all kinds of stories of what some of you call 'Hell,' and many people still believe them. According to these stories, Satan was in charge of Hell and was the boss of all sorts of demons, the mean little bastards that stoked the fires and tortured people who were sent there. The more terrifying and horrible it was, the better. There was some good that came out of believing such a place might await you after your Earthly bodies ceased to function; it made some people fearful enough that they were kinder to others and followed more closely those Ten Commandments that I reworked in the first few of our conversations.

"What you will experience after death is nothing like those horrific descriptions. What happens is simple. Your soul, as you call it, is nothing more than awareness of your continuing existence. This consciousness of self, minus your body, will meet with me, God, as most of you have chosen to call me. I will playback your life for you to relive. As you relive your life, you will experience all the joys, sorrows, physical pain, mental anguish, terror, suffering that your actions have caused your fellow human beings to endure. You will be made aware of and experience everything you did in your life, from the tiniest incident, which you may not even recall, to those which you remember well and for which you are now possibly ashamed and regretful.

"You will see how everything you did during your Earthly existence affected all other people the way the ripples in a still body of water emanate outward from a pebble dropped therein, every action good or bad, and how your actions rippled outward and affected all of humanity. You will be very surprised at how far those ripples went. From this you will learn. For what other purpose could I have given you existence except to learn? Whether it be the tiniest kind gesture or the most hateful and cruel deed, I will know why you did every deed. There is no escaping this end-of-life event, no matter what you claimed to believe throughout every moment of your time on Earth.

"I do, however, modify what suffering you will experience by considering what the circumstances were as you progressed through life: whether you learned, and whether you were sorry for what you did and changed your behavior toward your fellow human beings as a result. Remember, though, that there is no fooling me; I know when someone claims to be sorry only because he or she was caught. Some of you humans had parents who neglected and abused you. Some of you committed terrible acts because others threatened harm to you, your loved ones, or other people if you didn't follow their orders. I understand it all.

"In many cases your laws on Earth do not excuse your breaking them and will mete out punishment even though you did not know what you did was breaking a law. I, however, consider all that ever happened to you that shaped your personality and formed your behavior and actions toward your fellow human beings. In the lyrics of one of your songs there are these words: 'God bless little children who have not been taught to hate.' Think about this because it is important. Children learn to hate from watching the behavior of their parents or from being taught by other adults to hate certain people because of their skin color, ethnicity, religion, or some other reason that matters not at all to me. This negative 'rippling out effect' is the cause of many of the troubles on your Earth.

"My exposing you to all the pain and suffering caused by your behavior will be difficult for each of you to bear, but there is no escaping it. That is the only way you can learn. Some of you, including those who have not learned to love themselves, will not accept this learning process, but I know what I will do to ease your way through the learning process. I will also show each of you how the kindness you bestowed and the good things you did for your fellow human beings that brought joy and happiness to others.

You, Dwight, have always had this curiosity and fear about me since you were four years old and blurted out the word God and were made to feel ashamed, embarrassed, and fearful. In your childhood religious training, you learned and recited what your teachers and parents told you to learn and recite. You said that you believed what you were told was true and recited words about flattering me, hopefully preventing me from being angry with you and perhaps punishing you. You participated in the rituals and sang songs of how almighty, powerful, and merciful I am. This is what most 'religious' people consider worship and they believe that it pleases me; but it isn't what really matters.

You, Dwight, worshipped me in the way that really matters many times during your life without even realizing that you were doing so. Whenever you see, marvel, and are awed by the miracles of my creation, you are worshipping me, just as you are whenever you show kindness and concern for the pain another person may be suffering. You were worshipping me when you told the buyer whose daughter had cancer that you 'put in some words with the Big Boss.' You were worshipping me when you telephoned the woman who had lost a child, and when you spoke to the man wearing the turban. You did those things without any thought that you were worshipping me. You believed that you had done something worthwhile, and that is how it should be. There are millions of people who perform all sorts of kind acts as you did, sometimes very simple things such as a smile and a friendly, kind word. Pleasing me is so very simple, but many people think I want the elaborate rituals in which they participate. If participating gives them feelings of peace and helps them to treat their fellow humans in a kinder manner, then good for them.

"After this life playback, what happens then?" I asked Old One.

Old One responded again with a chuckle. "I knew you would ask, but that's one of your questions I won't answer. There must be unknowns for you humans to ponder, so you will continue to strive to learn by discovering the answers. The purpose of the playback of your lives is for you to learn. Each of you will go on learning. I give you no other choice. Although some of you will resist continuing to learn, you all will eventually continue with the learning process. There is a purpose and a goal for each of you, for all of humanity and for all other intelligent life in the universe. Each of you must strive to learn what that goal is and do what you must to reach it. That is the purpose of your existence. I will help in some ways, but other questions you must figure out for yourselves. Think about what I have just told you. Call me again when you are ready. I'm always around."

Chapter 26
Peace on Earth

Absolute quiet! I had parked the RV in a campground in Canyonlands National Park, Utah, near the confluence of the Colorado and Green rivers. This park, which is on a mesa, is called Island in the Sky. Describing our location as the "middle of nowhere" would be accurate as the town of Moab is thirty or forty miles distant. The night sky was totally black—no moon, only the stars, countless stars. I lay on a blanket, a small pillow cushioning my head, gazing upward at the stars; sometimes with my naked eyes, sometimes through binoculars. I picked out some of the best-known constellations: Ursa Major (the Great Bear), also known as the Big Dipper, and Ursa Minor (the Little Bear), the Little Dipper, in which Polaris, the North Star, is found. People throughout history learned to use Polaris to determine latitude and aid in navigation. I located Cassiopeia, which I remembered because to me it looked like the letter "W" or "M," depending upon the time of the year. I found the Pleiades with my naked eye, also called the Seven Sisters because of the seven closely grouped stars in the constellation Taurus. Then I looked at it through my binoculars, and it morphed into more stars than I ever could count and could hardly imagine. I thought of the beautiful images captured by the Hubble Space Telescope and of the time when Old One showed me flashes of the creation during our journey through time and space.

As I marveled at the fraction of the universe that I was able to observe, I asked, "What more do you have to say to me, Old One?"

Old One replied, "I'm going to tell you what you already actually know but need to be reminded of often. I want you to think of what a wonderful place your Earth could be if you humans would only stop being unkind and often cruel to one another. You people argue, fight and kill each other so often over which ideologies are correct and which of them please or do not please me. None of your religions have

185

it totally right. I repeat again: "I don't care about being told how great, wonderful, merciful and almighty I am. I don't care at all about this worship business. I have told you in our conversations that marveling and being awed by the natural world and being kind to one another is what I consider worship. When you feast your eyes on the beauty and behave with kindness and generosity towards your fellow humans, you are worshipping my creation, and that pleases me.

Powerful and arrogant figures in the many varied religions or political systems that exist on your Earth make the arrogant claim that their way is the only way and that all others are wrong. They persuade their followers that those who criticize their religion or political system of government must be punished—sometimes by hideous torture and death. The people who are in positions of power, either spiritual or political, can't allow people to express themselves freely because their ideas may loosen their grip on power. They know how freedom of thought, speech, or the written word threatens to bring down their lofty positions.

"So, why do they want power? They want power because it enables them to enslave people. People can be enslaved not only by being placed in chains but also by being forbidden to speak or write whatever they choose to. Those in power don't fool me when they justify their actions by claiming it is for the good of those over whom they rule. They crush free expression of thought and expression for their own benefit.

Think what your world would be like if people could travel to anywhere on Earth and discuss whatever political or religious beliefs they might hold without fear of punishment. As I have said before, I know that there are countless people on your Earth who pretend to follow a religion only because they fear punishment or ostracism from a social group.

"We have talked much," Old One said. "Sometimes I answered your questions, sometimes not. Sometimes I have told you things without your asking. I spoke to you not because you were certain that I exist but

186

because you asked me to. I knew you were thinking if you asked the Old One to speak to you, maybe you would get a response—if Old One existed. I'll speak to anyone who asks if they only consider it possible that I exist.

"Now, there have been people who have walked the Earth and done their best to spread the word of how freedom and peace can be achieved on Earth, and they did so, not to become powerful, or wealthy, but to live in such a way that when their lives were over they had contributed to the improvement of humanity. Here they are."

Human figures began to appear before me, as though materializing out of a mist. There were many, male and female: those I had heard of and others I didn't recognize. One by one, they appeared. Old One identified each one as they appeared; I had no way of knowing their identity because I had only seen pictures of some of them which came from an artist's mind. All those of whom I had heard appeared: Abraham, Buddha, Confucius, Dalai Lamas, Guru Nanak, Jesus, Lao Tzu, Mohammed, Native American spiritual leaders, and spiritual leaders from cultures of which I knew nothing.

They spoke as in one voice, one soft, yet grand, resonant, awesome chorus: "We all offered the same message—kindness and peace among all peoples. Don't do to others that which you wouldn't want done to yourself. Then, some who sought and attained power took our messages and corrupted them, twisting them for their own benefit; claiming their way was the only way. They often used force to spread their version of our message. Believe in one of us or all of us, but it is pointless to use force to make people pretend to believe; Old One knows what people truly believe." Then, gradually, they all faded away, dissolving back into the mists of time, back to eternity. And I knew Old One was always there whenever I might call—when circumstances were right.

Chapter 27
Wrapping It Up

I have told it all. I don't know if Old One really spoke to me, or if I imagined what I have written here. But whenever I asked Old One to converse with me, thoughts would form in my mind and that is what I have written here. No one in my family believes that I have conversed with God (Old One), but that doesn't bother me at all. We all have to figure out for ourselves "this God business" as I call it. What I have arrived at is very satisfying to me. If a Supreme Being created the universe and all that is in it, then it makes sense to me that that same Creator could have made it impossible for humans or any other intelligent life in the universe to prove or disprove Its existence. Was Old One actually conversing with me? I don't know. I told Old One this—that I still wasn't sure—and the thought that came back was this:

Don't worry about it. Remember, I don't get offended. You don't have everything figured out, but you're working on it and trying hard. That is all I expect from anyone.

I'm an old man, just recently past eighty-three years as I conclude my story. I'm a long way down the pathway of life, and the end could come at any moment or it may be some years away. I'm not afraid of death, but I do fear how I might die. I am fearful of pain, and there are ways of dying that I'm sure would be agonizing. But death itself holds no fear for me.

A writer by the name of Ernest K. Gann, who had been an airline pilot, an adventurer of sorts, and a writer, was interviewed late in his life. He was asked what his thoughts were as to his own demise, to which he replied: "That will be the greatest adventure!" That's how I look at my own departure. When this old body gives out, there will either be nothing or something. If it's nothing, why should one fear it?

Whichever way it turns out to be—the end or a new beginning after this life on Earth—I hope I have touched some people's lives in a positive way in this lifetime and have left this world in some way a little better.

When I said during one of our conversations that I am not afraid of Old One, the reply I received was as follows:

"Good, I don't want you to fear me. No one need fear me, but most of you humans do, and as your Henry David Thoreau wrote: 'The mass of men (people) lead lives of quiet desperation.' People create so much desperation for themselves, mostly because they don't love themselves. They spend much of their lives concerned with what others think about their physical appearance, dress, mental capacity, material possessions, and accomplishments. But all a person should be concerned about is whether they are considered to be a kind, honest, compassionate human being. Much of the "quiet desperation" people generate is because deep down, in their innermost thoughts, they are uncertain that there is a God. Because of that uncertainty, they worry that if God exists, they will be severely punished and sent to the Hell place; which you humans dreamed up.

"Humans need only fear their own actions. Remember that 'Hell' is a playback, in which you will experience the effect your life had on your fellow human beings, so you can learn. Each of you create your own 'Hell.' Don't sweat it! It's so very simple. Just be kind to your fellow human beings. You and I will meet sometime. Everyone will meet me when their time comes, even those who are certain that I don't exist, much to their surprise." Old One chuckled.

"And I will not be angry or displeased with those who have denied my existence. Remember, I don't have the anger and ego problems that so many of you humans have. When people meet with me, it will indeed be 'the greatest adventure' that each of you will ever experience."

Epilogue

I was flying the morning freight run to Port Angeles, Washington on a squally morning in mid-April: gusty wind and scattered rain showers. I had "turned the corner" near Port Townsend and was headed directly toward the Port Angeles airport. I flew in and out of rain showers but never in cloud. It was about 7:30 in the morning. I had checked in with the Whidbey Island air traffic controller and was just passing over Discovery Bay. There was a rain shower directly ahead when a break in the clouds behind me let the rising sunshine through. As the sunshine brightened, I looked ahead in awe. I was flying toward the exact center of triple, circular rainbows. Their colors were vivid—red, orange, yellow, green, blue, indigo and violet. Three, perfect, gorgeous concentric circles.

I stared, transfixed! I punched the radio transmit button and said to the Whidbey controller, "I can't believe this but I'm flying straight into the center of triple, circular rainbows."

The controller came back immediately with, "And I'll bet you don't have a camera." I didn't have a camera. The hole in the clouds in the east slowly closed; and the triple rainbow faded away—but it remains etched into my memory. My mind drifted to Old One, whose response came, "That was pretty cool wasn't it!"

I found the poem "High Flight" many years ago when I had only flown about one hundred hours. When my memoir was nearly finished I found it again and realized that it expresses the emotions I experienced after flying several thousand hours much later in life. It was composed by pilot officer John Gillespie Magee Jr. while flying over England at 30,000 feet in 1941. He was killed at age nineteen while serving with the Royal Canadian Air Force.

High Flight

Oh, I have slipped the surly bonds of earth

And danced the skies on laughter-silvered wings

Sunward I've climbed and joined the tumbling mirth

Of sun-split clouds—and done a hundred things

You have not dreamed of—wheeled and soared and swung

High in the sunlit silence: hovering there,

I've chased the shouting wind along and flung

My eager craft through footless halls of air.

Up, the long delirious burning blue

I've topped the windswept heights with easy grace.

Where never lark, or even eagle flew—

And while the silent lifting mind I've trod

The high un-trespassed sanctity of space

Put out my hand and touched—

The face of God

Acknowledgements

This book has taken about eighteen years to write. It began with short notes that I wrote to myself as I searched my collection of life-time memories. I'm old as I write this conclusion to my off and on search to figure out "this God business" as I call it. There have been many revisions and additions to this story as it progressed. Along the way I have mentioned it to various friends and acquaintances; some asked to read what I had written and I name those people here who have encouraged me to keep on writing and bring my story to a conclusion..

I first have to give credit to my wife Vera, of over sixty-four years, who put up with a writer without complaining about my leaving her without my company as I struggled with finding the elusive words that I was often seeking. She read many of the revisions along the way and was always honest with her opinion. She also put up with my being away from her often from before she arose in the morning to sometimes not getting home until very late evening during the years that I was flying.

My editor, Melanie Austin, was willing to work with a first time author who had never before attempted to write a book. I cannot find words to thank her enough. She never ceased to encourage me to continue, even when I sometimes became discouraged. She always found the right words to pull me out of a writer's "funk". Thank you Melanie for your help, encouragement and many kind words. This book would never have been completed without your guidance.

Thank you Michael Hill, for giving an old man the opportunity to fly airplanes for ten years late in the old man's life. I couldn't wait to get to my "job", I didn't consider it a job. But the idle time the flying job entailed gave me the time to put my thoughts together. That idle time was when my conversations with "Old One" began.

Thank you, Maryellen Elcock for reading some of my early efforts and urging me to keep on.

Thanks to my good neighbor, Gene Andersen who read a very early version and said, "keep on going."

Thank you, Ann Breen Metcalf, longtime friend of my sister Lueza, for reading a near finished manuscript and offering kind words of praise.

Thank you, Mike van Steenwyck for reading an early version and for your words of encouragement.

Thank you, Bob Welch for reading and offering kind words. We have known each other since we were kids, I guess that would be for a lifetime.

Thank you, Myles Gilbert, long-time friend, for reading, commenting and encouragement.

Thank you, Tristan Lockhart, for reading an excerpt and offering words of encouragement.

Thank you, Ms. Kaur, delightful Sikh lady, for reading a passage and saying kind words.

Thank you, Pam Linden, friend and once neighbor, for reading completely an almost finished manuscript and encouragement.

Thank you, Kim, who works at the Black Diamond, Washington Post Office. She happened to notice the title of my book when I was mailing a very early version and said she would like to read it. That very early version was quite a mess, various type fonts, misspellings, etc. It was a version that reflected what I had been advised to do when setting out to write: just let thoughts spill onto paper, go back to revise and polish later.

Made in the
USA
Lexington, KY